INTERNATIONAL DEVELOPMENT IN FOCUS

Skilled Migration
A Sign of Europe's Divide or Integration?

LAURENT BOSSAVIE, DANIEL GARROTE-SÁNCHEZ,
MATTIA MAKOVEC, AND ÇAĞLAR ÖZDEN

WORLD BANK GROUP

Contents

Map

Tables

Preface

Despite the strong income convergence among countries of the European Union (EU) in recent decades, large socioeconomic disparities remain between EU countries and regions. These persistent differences create strong incentives for workers to migrate to take advantage of these gaps, a process enabled by the free movement of labor within the EU. Although migration results from these economic and social imbalances between countries, there has been debate on whether migration also exacerbates economic disparities. The public debate on migration in Europe, however, has often been motivated by ideology rather than empirical evidence, preventing an informed discussion on the costs and benefits of workers' cross-border mobility.

Skilled Migration: A Sign of Europe's Divide or Integration? aims to contribute to an evidence-based policy debate on migration in Europe. Using rigorous data analyses and a review of the existing literature, the report takes a careful look at the trends, determinants, and impacts of high-skilled migration within the EU over the past two decades and discusses the main policy implications.

The report's main thesis is that high-skilled migration, whether internal or international, is largely a symptom rather than a cause of the persisting gaps in labor market and educational opportunities, productivity, welfare, and the quality of institutions across regions. The findings show that the remaining socioeconomic disparities between European countries—in particular, wage differentials—are key determinants of migration flows within the EU. Thus, as a result, labor migration—especially skilled labor migration—has been growing rapidly in the past two decades. As of 2018, almost one-third of total migrants in the EU had a tertiary education. When considering migrants from the EU15 Member States (the EU member countries before 2004: Austria, Belgium, Denmark, Finland, France, Germany, Greece, Ireland, Italy, Luxembourg, the Netherlands, Portugal, Spain, Sweden, and the United Kingdom), the share of migrants with tertiary education rises to 45 percent, a dramatic increase compared to the 25 percent reported in 2001.

This report offers a comprehensive analysis of the benefits and costs of skilled migration for both sending and receiving countries in the EU and investigates the potential implications of a large outflow of highly qualified workers on the economies of the sending regions. The analysis shows that the impacts of migration are far more complex than commonly understood. The effects of migration depend on multiple factors, including the extent of the complementarity and substitutability of migrants and natives in receiving countries and the capacity of sending regions to realize the benefits from return or circular migration and other knowledge spillovers. The report highlights that migration within the EU is not always permanent but is often a temporary phenomenon. As a result, while countries incur short-term costs resulting from the departure of part of their skilled labor force, there can be multiple benefits associated with the circulation of labor if migrants ultimately return home.

The report also shows that there is potential to further increase the benefits and reduce the costs of migration for both sending and receiving countries in the EU. It proposes policy actions to address the various costs that migration induces among different skill groups within both migrant-sending and -receiving regions, both in the short and long runs. While some of these policy actions can be taken unilaterally by sending or receiving countries, others require improving cross-country coordination to better unlock the overall benefits of migration within the EU.

After two years of the COVID-19 (coronavirus) pandemic, the EU economies are slowly recovering. Cross-border labor migration will play a critical role in this recovery. This report aims to be a useful resource for governments, development partners, and policy makers throughout the EU to unlock the full potential of migration for both sending and receiving countries.

Acknowledgments

This report has been prepared under the guidance and supervision of the World Bank's Elisabetta Capannelli (former country manager of Croatia), Cem Mete (practice manager, Social Protection and Jobs, Europe and Central Asia [HECSP]), and Lars Sondergaard (lead economist and program leader, Human Development, European Union). It represents the main deliverable of the project "Migration and Brain Drain in the European Union" and has been authored by a team led by Mattia Makovec (senior economist and team task leader, HECSP), and including Laurent Bossavie (economist, HECSP), Daniel Garrote-Sánchez (consultant, HECSP), and Çağlar Özden (lead economist, Development Economics Research Group).

The authors gratefully acknowledge the comments received on an earlier draft of this report by the peer reviewers: Jamele Rigolini (lead economist and program leader, Human Development, Western Balkans), Indhira Santos (senior economist, Social Protection and Jobs, and global lead for Jobs and Skills), and Erwin Tiongson (Georgetown University). The authors are also grateful to Fadia Saadah (regional director, Human Development, Europe and Central Asia) for the helpful guidance provided at the inception of this work, and for the suggestions received from Donato De Rosa (lead economist, Macroeconomics, Trade, and Investment, Europe and Central Asia), Tommaso Frattini (University of Milan), Josip Funda (senior economist, Macroeconomics, Trade, and Investment, Europe and Central Asia), Harry Patrinos (practice manager, Education, Europe and Central Asia), Panu Poutvaara (University of Munich), Giuseppe Russo (University of Salerno), Pia Schneider (lead economist, Health, Nutrition and Population), Ana Simundza (research analyst, World Bank Office, Zagreb), Emilia Skrok (senior economist and program leader, Equitable Growth, Finance, and Institutions, European Union), and Mauro Testaverde (senior economist, HECSP). The authors would also like to thank Dora Bagic (consultant, Finance, Competitiveness, and Innovation) and Andrea Bernini (University of Oxford) for their excellent contributions. We owe a special thank you to Cindy Fisher and Mark McClure of the World Bank's Publishing Program for their great support, professionalism, and patience throughout the publishing process.

About the Authors

Laurent Bossavie is an economist in the World Bank's Social Protection and Jobs Global Practice, Europe and Central Asia Region. His main areas of expertise are labor economics and the economics of migration. His work explores the role of labor and migration policies in shaping the labor market outcomes of workers in both advanced economies and developing countries. His research on these topics has been published in leading peer-reviewed journals in labor economics, including the *Journal of Human Resources*, and as World Bank analytical reports and books. He holds a PhD in economics from the European University Institute in Florence, Italy.

Daniel Garrote-Sánchez is a consultant in the World Bank's Social Protection and Jobs Global Practice, Europe and Central Asia Region. His areas of research include the drivers and impact of labor migration and forced displacement in sending and receiving countries, integration in host communities, and return migration. Before joining the World Bank, he worked for the Lebanese Center of Policy Studies, the Ministry of Labor of Saudi Arabia, and the Central Bank of Spain. He holds a master's degree in public administration and international development from the Harvard Kennedy School and a BA in economics and law from Carlos III University.

Mattia Makovec is a senior economist in the World Bank's Social Protection and Jobs Global Practice, Europe and Central Asia Region. He leads operations, analytic activities, and policy dialogue on jobs, social protection, and migration, in particular in Turkey and European Union Member States. Previously, he worked at the World Bank Office in Jakarta, Indonesia, and held positions at Essex University, the University of Chile, and the Ministry of Labor in Chile. Mattia has a PhD in economics from Bocconi University in Milan and a master's degree in economics from University College London.

Çağlar Özden is a lead economist in the World Bank's Development Economics Research Group. A Turkish national, he is a fellow of the IZA Institute of Labor Economics, Centre for Research and Analysis of Migration, and Economic Research Forum. His research explores the nexus of globalization of product and labor markets, government policies, and economic development. He has edited three books and published numerous papers in leading academic journals such as the *American Economic Review* and the *Economic Journal*. His current research projects explore the determinants and patterns of global labor mobility; impacts of migrants on the destination labor market outcomes; links between migration, trade, and foreign direct investment flows; medical brain drain; and links between aging and global economic integration. He holds undergraduate degrees in economics and industrial engineering from Cornell University and a PhD in economics from Stanford University.

Executive Summary

MIGRATION AS A SYMPTOM OF EUROPE'S ECONOMIC DISPARITIES

During the last several decades, there has been rapid income integration and convergence across EU countries, although persistent gaps remain in wages and employment opportunities, human capital, welfare and social protection, governance, and quality of institutions. These gaps not only exist between Western EU countries (EU15) and the New Member States of the EU (NMS13), but also within countries, and more broadly between more developed and lagging regions across Europe. Against this backdrop, high-skilled migration emerges as a symptom rather than a driver of the large intra-EU disparities in productivity, education, labor market outcomes, and other underlying structural factors.

THE EXTENT OF ECONOMIC MIGRATION IN THE EUROPEAN UNION

The European countries' economies have experienced profound changes since the early 1990s, in the context of global economic integration and increasing international migration. The number of foreign-born residents in the European Union (EU) has more than doubled since 1990, reaching 60 million in 2019. As a result, the EU hosts close to one-quarter of all the world's migrants. A sizable share of migrants in the EU are from other EU member countries (21 million). Still, intra-EU mobility remains lower than in Australia or the United States, given the presence of larger mobility barriers, such as language (Ridao-Cano and Bodewig 2018). Immigration has been largely concentrated in the Western EU countries, where more than 90 percent of all immigrants to the EU reside. From the perspective of the countries of origin, emigration rates from the Eastern EU countries since their EU accession have rapidly increased, accounting for more than 15 percent of the total population in Romania, Bulgaria, and Lithuania. By destination area, most Eastern EU emigrants migrate to the

Western EU countries, whereas Western EU emigrants remain within the region or emigrate to non-EU countries, mostly more developed non-EU OECD countries.

The rise in skilled migration to the EU has been even more pronounced over the past 15 years, reaching 13 million of tertiary-educated migrants in 2019. By region of origin, the education levels of migrants from all regions increased, especially among Western EU migrants who already had higher education levels in the early 2000s. Reflecting geographical disparities in productivity, skill shortages, and skill-specific wage premiums across the EU, high-skilled migrants are disproportionately concentrated in certain countries and in certain regions within countries in Europe. In line with the upward trends in educational attainment, the share of migrants in the EU working in nonroutine occupations has risen, in some cases faster than among the overall EU population (for example, for migrants from Western EU countries).

High-skilled migrants in the EU tend to be younger than the average migrant population. A higher share of tertiary-educated migrants from Eastern EU countries are women, while there is broader gender parity among skilled migrants from the Western EU. Skilled migrants tend to self-select into occupations with a different task content than natives. Occupational downgrading is a relevant phenomenon, which particularly affects qualified migrants from Eastern EU countries. When working in high-skilled occupations, migrants tend to perform more analytical tasks, while natives are concentrated in communication-oriented tasks. Information and communication technology represents one of the largest shares of occupation for educated migrants.

DRIVERS OF MIGRATION WITHIN THE EUROPEAN UNION

Wage and employment differentials between EU countries are strongly correlated with migration flows in the region. Although parts of the gaps in labor earnings are due to differences in education across countries, several studies have found that workers with similar skills can have large disparities in productivity and earnings depending on the country where they reside—which is called the place premium. The type and quality of employment opportunities have been shaped by technological change and automation, which have changed the geography of jobs over time. Prosperous regions with greater opportunities for finding high-quality nonroutine cognitive jobs have attracted more highly educated migrants. Within the EU, free mobility between countries allows migrants to take advantage of these differentials and move for better opportunities.

Demographic patterns and social, institutional, and governance factors also play important roles in migration flows. For example, the literature has found that the presence of migrant networks of the same nationality in a given country attracts newer cohorts of migrants (Clark, Hatton, and Williamson 2007). The relative quality of public services, the generosity of the welfare system, and employment protection legislation also are push-and-pull factors for migration. In addition, evidence suggests that corruption plays an important role in both increasing emigration (when corruption is higher in migrant-sending countries relative to receiving ones) and deterring immigration (when corruption in receiving countries is higher with respect to sending ones), a factor that particularly affects high-skilled workers.

THE IMPACT OF MIGRATION ON RECEIVING COUNTRIES

Existing evidence generally shows a positive impact of immigration on the economic growth of European migrant-receiving countries, although the result depends on the skill composition of migrants—with high-skilled migration producing more positive effects—and on the characteristics of destination countries (for example, the composition of the workforce). The positive contribution of high-skilled migration to growth is observed through different channels: increasing the stock and variety and the quality of human capital, raising the productivity of the economy, and incentivizing the adoption of new technologies and stimulating capital accumulation. Immigration has also been an engine for population growth in Western EU countries for the last several decades. From 1995 and 2017, net migration inflows accounted for close to 80 percent of the total population growth in these countries, compensating for the weak natural growth rate observed during this period. Given that immigrants in Western EU countries are, on average, younger and more likely to be of working age compared with natives, the migration phenomenon has partially alleviated the aging process in these economies. Nevertheless, the current pace of immigration would not suffice to prevent population aging in Western Europe in the coming decades.

In the labor market of migrant-receiving countries, the empirical evidence has shown that immigration has had small but generally positive effects on wages and employment of native-born adults. The EU enlargements in 2004, 2007, and 2013, which led to a larger influx of migrants from Eastern EU to Western EU countries, did not bring about relevant changes in labor earnings of the native population. On the contrary, immigration has generally helped address skill and labor shortages in specific regions and occupations (World Bank 2018). Behind its generally positive impact, migration can displace or reduce the wages of certain groups of native workers with profiles more similar to migrants' in the short run, while in the longer run natives tend to adjust and move to other occupations. Accounting for the costs and benefits of migration, studies in most EU countries show a broadly neutral or slightly positive fiscal impact of immigrants in the host economies. Skilled migrants, in particular, tend to be net contributors to tax and social insurance systems in destination countries (OECD 2013).

THE IMPACT OF MIGRATION ON SENDING COUNTRIES AND THE POTENTIAL FOR RETURN MIGRATION

In the short run, emigration of high-skilled workers can have a negative impact on productivity of workers that stay in the country of origin, slowing capital acquisition and innovation. This effect has been found in certain Eastern European countries (Anelli et al. 2019; Giesing and Laurentsyeva 2017). Migration has also exacerbated the ongoing process of aging and population and labor force decline in migrant-sending Eastern EU countries. In terms of human capital, emigration of high-skilled workers also reduces, in the short run, the average level of skills in the country. This can create shortages among qualified professionals such as doctors in migrant-sending regions of the EU. During the last decade, the outflows of physicians from Eastern and Southern EU countries to Western EU ones have been sizable, accounting, respectively, for 0.7 percent and 1.5 percent of the total stock of doctors in each region at its peak in 2014.

In the labor market, emigration had small effects on the wages of those who remained in the country of origin. These aggregate effects mask important variations across groups, as wages of workers with similar skills to those who migrate tend to increase given the reduced competition, while the opposite is true for those with complementary skills. In net terms, emigration, in particular that of high-skilled workers, reduces the tax base and the capacity of governments to raise revenues.

In the medium term, migration to regions with higher productivity and job opportunities can facilitate a more efficient allocation of labor across EU regions, reducing unemployment rates in areas with more limited labor demand. Reducing unemployment pressures can particularly benefit youth. In spite of the short-term reduction in human capital, emigration can incentivize educational investments in the medium term. The opportunities for higher wages overseas and increased internal demand can incentivize workers to obtain further education, potentially reverting the "brain drain" phenomenon to a "brain gain." However, net gains in human capital accumulation can be obtained only if a large enough number of newly educated individuals do not migrate overseas or end up returning home and if education capacity expands to accommodate the increased demand. The expansion in the supply of education has not occurred in all Eastern EU countries and, when it has, it has generated an additional fiscal cost for sending countries. Understanding why the supply of education responds more effectively to high-skilled emigration in some Eastern EU countries than in others has important policy implications. Overall, the stock of doctors in Eastern EU countries has risen despite the outflows of migrant doctors, although the increase in the supply has not caught up with the larger demand stemming from population aging and the related increase in the demand for health care services. Emigration also benefits sending countries through international remittances, which provide a key stabilization role for the economy and vital supplementary income to households, in particular at the lower end of the income distribution. On the other hand, remittances can dampen the incentives to work among households with migrant family members.

In the longer run, emigration to countries with better governance and institutions can shape migrants' attitudes and may contribute to improving social, economic, and political institutions in home countries. Emigration also promotes global social and professional networks, potentially reducing international transaction costs and facilitating trade, foreign direct investment, and knowledge spillovers between migrants' home and host countries. When returning home, migrants bring back productive skills that enhance the productivity of the economy. The incidence of return migration varies by the educational attainment of migrants, country of origin, and country of destination. In general, high-skilled migration from Western EU countries exhibits a high degree of circularity, with two in five migrants returning home within a decade. On the other hand, Eastern EU countries face more difficulties in attracting back their talented residents, given the persistence of challenges and drivers that led skilled migrants to move out of the country in the first place. Return rates are particularly low among Eastern EU high-skilled migrants who moved to non-EU OECD countries, such as the United States, Canada, and Australia. When emigration turns permanent, lagging regions are unable to benefit from this important aspect of migration circularity. Among those who return to their home countries, evidence shows that migrants from Eastern EU countries earn higher wages when having a salaried job and are more likely to become self-employed, generating new activities and potentially creating more jobs.

THE IMPLICATIONS OF COVID-19 FOR MIGRANTS IN THE EUROPEAN UNION

The COVID-19 pandemic has severely limited mobility, reducing labor supply in the EU and globally, while the increased uncertainty associated with the duration of the pandemic and reduced consumption levels dampened labor demand. As a result, employment in the EU fell in 2020. The empirical evidence shows that, at any level of education, migrants face greater vulnerabilities to COVID-19-related shocks compared to natives, in terms of risks of job and earnings losses. Migrants are also more exposed to COVID-19-related health risks. The implications and exposure, however, are highly asymmetric across migrant groups, with migrants from Eastern EU countries being more vulnerable than those from Western EU countries. Across skill levels, high-skilled migrants are less vulnerable than those with lower education, which could affect the composition and profile of return migrants. Although migration data post-COVID are still not available, the potential reduction in the stock of migrants due to employment losses can have sizable effects on remittances in the region.

POLICY RECOMMENDATIONS

The evidence compiled in this report highlights the asymmetric costs and benefits of migration in both sending and receiving countries, which vary in the short, medium, and long terms, and across different groups of the population. In a context of free mobility across member states and persistent economic disparities, policies in EU countries should focus on better managing migration flows and promote brain circulation, by tapping international networks and know-how rather than only trying to prevent the drain of human capital in the first place. Furthermore, policies to enhance return migration and limit the emigration of high-skilled professionals are complementary and require tackling relevant underlying structural social, economic and political challenges.

In order to reduce the short-term costs of labor mobility in sending regions, policy makers need to address barriers in the domestic labor market to increase its relative attractiveness vis-à-vis more prosperous regions. For example, ensuring that employment protection legislation is flexible enough so it does not stifle job creation, especially among high-skilled new entrants into the labor market, can reduce, at least partially, the incentives to emigrate and enhance return migration. More broadly, strengthening domestic institutions and governance, safety nets, and welfare systems in sending regions can also curb migration outflows and promote return migration. Sending regions may also open the domestic labor market to non-EU migrants to import necessary skills when and to the extent the political context allows it.

In the longer run, migrant-sending countries and regions have a larger menu of policy options at their disposal in order to maximize the benefits of migration and brain circulation and to enhance the availability of human capital demanded in the domestic labor market. These policy options can be divided between those that can be implemented independently by either receiving or sending countries and those that need coordination between governments.

Among the policies that can be implemented independently, one option is to reform tertiary education financing systems in sending countries to address the fiscal losses associated with the emigration of graduates from publicly funded universities. Income-contingent loans (ICLs), by which students repay the loan only once their income exceeds a certain threshold, emerge as a potential instrument to ensure the fiscal sustainability of the education system as well as equity in accessing tertiary education across income levels. To prevent difficulties in loan repayment of emigrants, ICL contracts could be designed to make loan repayments feasible and tax deductible in destination countries (Poutvaara 2004). Other options for reform of the tertiary education financing system include progressive tuition programs accompanied by income tax credits and deductions for university graduates who decide to remain working in the domestic labor market, especially for occupations in high demand. Another important aspect to enhance the overall benefits of migration is the need to better monitor the supply and demand of skills in sending countries and to adjust the quantity and quality of the supply of university majors and careers accordingly. In order to incentivize the return of high-skilled migrants, sending countries may introduce tax breaks and incentives in specific strategic sectors and reintegration programs to support migrants throughout the process of job search, connecting them to employment opportunities and easing institutional and bureaucratic barriers. Given the higher propensity of returned migrants to be self-employed and entrepreneurs, strengthening the business environment in sending countries can ease their transition back to their home labor markets. In turn, receiving countries could speed up the integration process of immigrants in host labor markets by investing in integration and host language training programs.

A second group of policy options require coordination between sending and receiving countries. EU countries can develop an EU-wide labor demand system to assess shortages of skills and occupations in different regions, where education supply targets in each area not only take into consideration prospective demand but also migration flows. In order to mitigate skill waste and promote integration, EU countries could strengthen their coordination in validating the foreign credentials of other member states. Global skill partnerships between sending and receiving countries can address issues of brain drain and financial burden in the former and improve skill matches in the latter. Countries still have room to expand migrants' access to social protection by guaranteeing the full portability of pensions, unemployment, and health care benefits, and to reduce the costs of remittances that would benefit migrant households by resorting to new technologies (for example, mobile payments).

Finally, in order to design better evidence-based policies, there is a need to improve the quality, depth, and frequency of data collection on migration. At destination, besides ad hoc migration modules, surveys lack detailed information on immigrants' socioeconomic characteristics and experiences in the country of origin. In sending countries, household surveys have even more difficulty capturing current emigrants. Most countries lack surveys with modules surveying households on members currently living abroad. There is also a need to develop more detailed ad hoc surveys on migrant households to identify migration trajectories following migrants over time and collecting retrospective information on the history of migration and employment. And there is a strong need to better observe labor mobility across EU countries in national administrative data sources, and to match them with other administrative databases, both domestically and across countries.

REFERENCES

Anelli, Massimo, Gaetano Basso, Giuseppe Ippedico, and Giovanni Peri. 2019. "Youth Drain, Entrepreneurship, and Innovation." NBER Working Paper 26055 (July), National Bureau of Economic Research, Cambridge, MA.

Clark, X., T. J. Hatton, and J. G. Williamson. 2007. "Explaining US Immigration, 1971–1998." *Review of Economics and Statistics* 89 (2): 359–73.

Giesing, Yvonne, and Nadzeya Laurentsyeva. 2017. "Firms Left Behind: Emigration and Firm Productivity." CESifo Working Paper 6815 (December), Munich Society for the Promotion of Economic Research, Center for Economic Studies, Ludwig Maximilian University and Ifo Institute for Economic Research, Munich.

OECD (Organisation for Economic Co-operation and Development). 2013. "The Fiscal Impact of Immigration in OECD Countries." *International Migration Outlook 2013*, 125–89. Paris: OECD Publishing.

Poutvaara, Panu. 2004. "Educating Europe: Should Public Education Be Financed with Graduate Taxes or Income-Contingent Loans?" *CESifo Economic Studies* 50 (4): 663–84.

Ridao-Cano, Cristobal, and Christian Bodewig. 2018. "Growing United: Upgrading Europe's Convergence Machine." World Bank Report on the European Union, World Bank, Washington, DC.

World Bank. 2018. *Moving for Prosperity: Global Migration and Labor Markets*. Policy Research Report. Washington, DC: World Bank.

Abbreviations

CEPII	Centre d'Études Prospectives et d'Informations Internationales
DIOC	Database on Immigrants in OECD and Non-OECD Countries
ECA	Eastern Europe and Central Asia
EFTA	European Free Trade Association
EU	European Union
GDP	gross domestic product
ICL	income-contingent loan
ICT	information and communication technology
ISCO	International Standard Classification of Occupations
LAC	Latin America and the Caribbean
LFS	Labour Force Survey (EU)
NMS	New Member States (of the EU)
NUTS	Nomenclature of Territorial Units for Statistics
OECD	Organisation for Economic Co-operation and Development
PPML	Poisson pseudo-maximum likelihood estimator
PPP	purchasing power parity
SGIE	Secretary General of Immigration and Emigration (Spain)
SPS	social protection spending

Introduction

This report was prepared at the request of the Croatia World Bank Country Office in the context of Croatia's presidency of the Council of the European Union (EU) from January 1 to June 30, 2020.[1] The findings were intended to inform preparatory meetings of the Council around the topic of skilled migration in the EU, but the meetings were suspended because of the COVID-19 (coronavirus) pandemic. Nonetheless, the report was completed with the aim to generate evidence and inform policy dialogue in other EU countries with active World Bank engagements (for example, Bulgaria, Poland, and Romania), for which the out-migration of skilled workers and tertiary-educated young cohorts is a particularly relevant phenomenon and often a matter of concern for policy makers and various stakeholders in the society.

The report examines the migration trends, drivers, and impacts among skilled workers within the EU during the last two decades using original data analysis as well as an in-depth literature review. The study assesses the benefits and costs of skilled migration in the short run and the long run, and, while covering issues pertinent for both sending and receiving countries, it emphasizes the potential implications of a large outflow of highly qualified workers for the economies of the main sending regions. The audience for this work consists of policy makers in both migrant-sending and migrant-receiving EU member countries, EU institutions, and international organizations. On the basis of the analysis carried out, the report formulates policy recommendations with the aim of addressing the various costs that migration induces among groups within both migrant-sending and migrant-receiving regions and of improving cross-country coordination to better unlock the overall benefits of migration.

Although Member States have experienced relatively rapid income convergence and economic integration since the EU's enlargement, the EU is still characterized by persistent socioeconomic gaps across different regions along several dimensions. First are the labor market gaps arising from differences in wages and the quality of job opportunities, which are exacerbated by rapid technological change and the shifting nature of jobs. Second are the gaps in the stock of human capital caused by persistent differences in the quality and quantity of education available. Third are the gaps in welfare and social protection systems, and finally in the quality of institutions and governance. These gaps exist not only between the East and the West but also between the North and the South or within individual countries with large structural imbalances. In other words, these gaps occur between prospering and lagging regions across all of Europe.

The report highlights that high-skilled migration, both internal and international, is largely a symptom rather than a cause of the large labor market, educational, and productivity gaps and of other underlying structural factors. Labor mobility is a rational economic response to large differences in opportunities. Free movement within the EU enables workers and firms to take advantage of these gaps by enhancing the reallocation of workers from low- to high-productivity sectors and regions. The process, however, can generate winners and losers, depending on the complementarity and substitutability between migrants and natives and on the capacity of sending regions to realize benefits from return or circular migration and other knowledge spillovers. In addition to mostly one-way migration from lagging regions to more prosperous ones, there is also a sizable amount of two-way mobility between richer countries and regions.[2]

Migrant-receiving regions tend to benefit from migration in different ways. Migration contributes to population growth in the presence of stagnating fertility rates and otherwise naturally declining population levels. It increases the stock, variety, and quality of human capital. It improves public finances because migrants, particularly highly skilled migrants, tend to be younger and higher-wage workers, and thus net contributors to tax and social insurance systems. It addresses demand shortages, mostly in services, by meeting the needs of an aging population.

From the perspective of sending countries and regions, skilled emigration produces both costs and benefits, which vary in the short run and the long run. In the short run, population and labor force shortages, which might be already occurring because of aging and low fertility rates, are exacerbated, worsening the gap between prospering and lagging regions. Human capital stock shrinks in the short run, especially in critical sectors with high external demand, and internal shortages increase among qualified professionals (for example, doctors and information technology professionals). However, emigration may alleviate unemployment pressures in sending regions, it incentivizes human capital accumulation in response to rising external and internal demand, and it brings back a flow of international remittances with potential benefits for poverty reduction. The incentivizing effect on human capital accumulation, however, might not solve the problem of sending countries that have constraints on education capacity or where costs are borne by the public sector. In the long run, the benefits of migration for sending regions depend critically on whether these regions manage to capitalize potential productivity-enhancing knowledge transfers through circular and return migration.

The report discusses the policy options available in the short run and the long run to enhance the benefits of skilled migration, as well as to address the associated losses, especially from the standpoint of human capital policies in sending countries. Because it is unrealistic to think about curbing migration flows without creating better economic opportunities and amenities in sending regions, policies aimed at stimulating the demand side of the labor market in sending countries and regions might be more effective at containing brain drain at the margin. Policies designed to improve the supply of human capital and to remove the structural gaps between sending and receiving regions will have effects only in the medium and long runs. Given the unequal burdens linked with migration, the report discusses various education financing policies to address fiscal losses associated with emigration, such as income-contingent loans and global skill partnerships between sending and receiving regions that can generate benefits for all participants.

Given the current context of COVID-19 and its expected impacts on labor mobility, the report briefly discusses the implications of the COVID-19 crisis among skilled migrants from the perspective of both countries of destination and countries of origin. However, a full treatment of the effect of the COVID-19 pandemic on skilled migration is beyond the purpose of this work and is left to future research. This is largely because, when the report was completed, limited data were available to assess how COVID-19 affected migrants' labor market outcomes and shaped the mobility decisions of potential migrants.

Finally, the scope of the report is limited to the economic impact of high-skilled migration. It does not analyze other cultural, sociological, or political aspects. The public sentiments of citizens toward migration in receiving countries have shaped migration policy in the EU and might have led to more push-back that negatively affected the potential benefits of migration, as recently highlighted in the case of Brexit. However, the concerns of policy makers and voters in receiving countries seem to be more highly concentrated on refugees and low-skilled migrants. Given that the focus of the report is to support a technical discussion of the issues involved in the drain on human capital in lagging regions, such issues are not considered. Still, it is important to weigh the relevant implications of Brexit in future migration flows of skilled workers in Europe.[3]

NOTES

1. Given the period in which the task started, and the data available at the time, throughout the report the authors consider the European Union as formed by its 28 Member States as of January 1, 2020, before the withdrawal of the United Kingdom (Brexit).
2. For example, according to United Nations Department of Economic and Social Affairs data from 2019, there are 442,000 Irish living in the United Kingdom and 293,000 British in Ireland, 238,000 Austrians residing in Germany and 264,000 Germans in Austria, and 348,000 Germans living in the United Kingdom and 99,000 British in Germany.
3. After Germany, the United Kingdom was the second-largest EU receiving country for high-skilled EU migrants as of 2018, hosting 1.3 million individuals.

1 Migration as a Symptom of Europe's Economic Disparities

Europe has undergone a remarkable process of income convergence and economic integration between East and West since the 2004 European Union (EU) fifth wave of enlargement. The European economies that joined the EU in 2004 have experienced impressive growth in per capita income, which has contributed to a reduction in income disparities between the East and the West. Sustained growth, improved governance, economic reform, trade expansion and integration, and capital and labor mobility have spurred the development of the 13 New Member States (the NMS13) joining the EU in 2004, 2007, and 2013.[1] On average, in the NMS13, real gross domestic product (GDP) grew by 3.4 percent annually following EU accession, compared with 0.8 percent among the EU15.[2] Average GDP per capita rose by 59 percent across the NMS13 in 2003–18, compared with an average of 11 percent among the EU15. Adjusted for purchasing power standards, average GDP per capita in the NMS13 reached 71 percent of the EU28 average in 2018, up from 49 percent in 2003.[3] In 2018, nine countries of the NMS13 recorded GDP per capita above 70 percent of the EU average, against only four countries in 2003 (figure 1.1).

As of 2018, all countries of the NMS13 except the latest members to join the EU (Bulgaria, Croatia, and Romania) exhibited higher GDP per capita than the two poorest countries among the EU15 (Greece and Portugal). In contrast, only Cyprus and Slovenia had a higher GDP per capita than Greece and Portugal in 2003.[4]

Despite these trends, there are still important income gaps between the countries in Western Europe and those in Eastern Europe. A comparison of incomes in the NMS13 and the EU15 shows that the average GDP per capita in the NMS13 represented only 62 percent of the average GDP per capita in the EU15 in 2018 and that, among half the NMS13, the corresponding ratio fell below 60 percent.

Contrary to the overall convergence in incomes across EU countries, income disparities within countries have been rising, suggesting that gaps persist between prospering and lagging regions. The subnational dimension of income disparity within the EU is also important. An examination of income convergence across regions indicates that the poorest regions experienced stronger growth in per capita income following the EU enlargement, which is a sign of convergence. However, whereas the between-country component of income

FIGURE 1.1

GDP per capita, EU Member States, 2003 and 2018

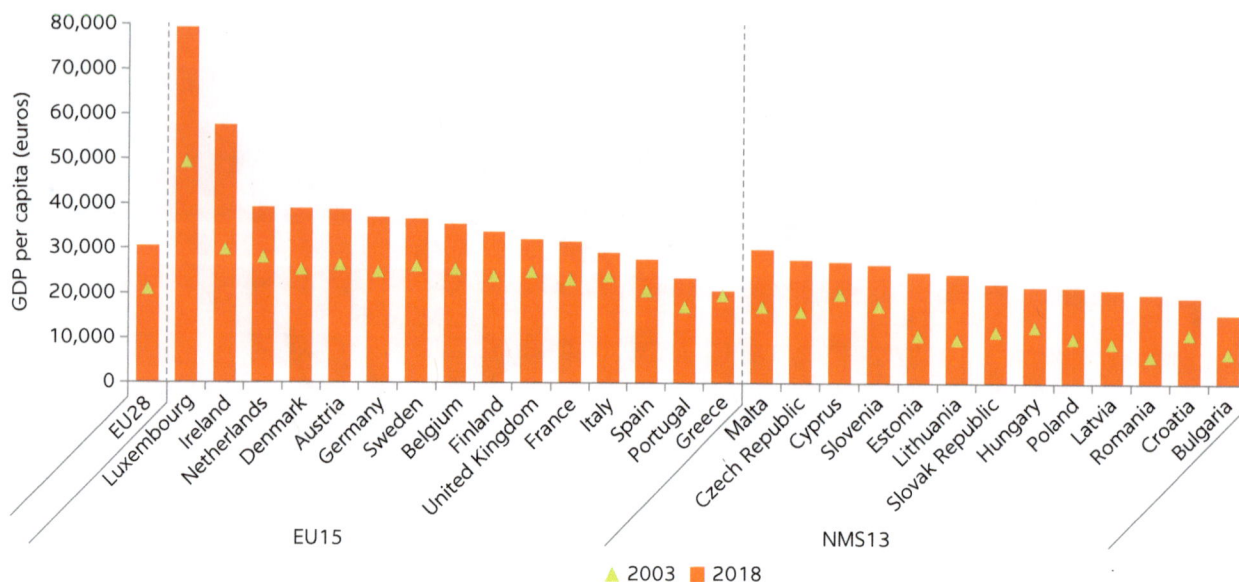

Source: World Bank elaborations based on data from Eurostat.

Note: GDP per capita values are purchasing power adjusted. EU15 = European Union members before 2004; EU28 = EU15 + NMS13; NMS13 = New Member States joining in 2004, 2007, and 2013.

inequality, measured by the coefficient of variation of GDP per capita across Nomenclature of Territorial Units for Statistics 2 (NUTS 2) regions, has declined since the early 2000s (though there was a reverse trend in the aftermath of the 2008–09 financial crisis), the within-country component of income disparity across regions has risen steadily (figure 1.2).[5] This is evidence of important income gaps not only between the West and the East but also between prospering and lagging regions within countries.

Technological change, globalization, and the shifting nature of jobs are contributing to divergence in productivity between firms and regions. In the past decade, productivity differentials have been widening both across countries and across regions within countries (Ridao-Cano and Bodewig 2018). It has been argued that technological change and globalization have exacerbated the increased divergence in productivity and wages among firms (OECD 2017). The most efficient firms have been able to take advantage of technological change and experienced large productivity gains, whereas others are lagging (Ridao-Cano and Bodewig 2018). In addition, technological change and globalization are making jobs more skill intensive, resulting in rising inequality between high- and low-skilled workers in the EU. Per capita labor income has gradually become more unequally distributed in most EU countries since the 1990s, a trend that intensified after 2008, particularly among countries in southeastern Europe (except Romania), where labor income inequality is already the highest.

Disparities in wage levels and job opportunities are also large. Average wage differentials between Western and Eastern Europe, though declining, remain large, especially among workers with tertiary education, thereby becoming a key determinant of skilled migration from east to west. A young graduate from Bulgaria or Romania who is working in Austria or the

FIGURE 1.2

Convergence of regional GDP per capita and inequality decomposition

a. Convergence, GDP per capita, NUTS 2 European regions

b. Decomposition, coefficient of variation

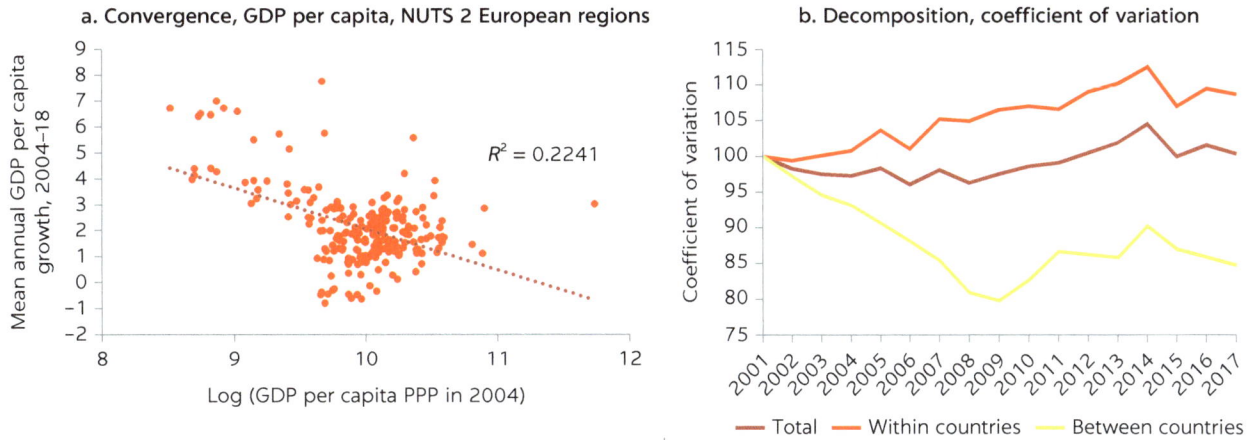

$R^2 = 0.2241$

Source: World Bank elaborations based on data from Eurostat.
Note: The coefficient of variation of GDP per capita is equal to the standard deviation of GDP per capita across countries, divided by the average GDP per capita in the EU28. EU28 = full European Union membership before departure of United Kingdom; NUTS 2 = Nomenclature of Territorial Units for Statistics 2; PPP = purchasing power parity.

FIGURE 1.3

Average wages among high-skilled workers in the European Union, by country of employment

a. Monthly earnings, EU15, 2016

b. Monthly earnings, NMS13, 2016

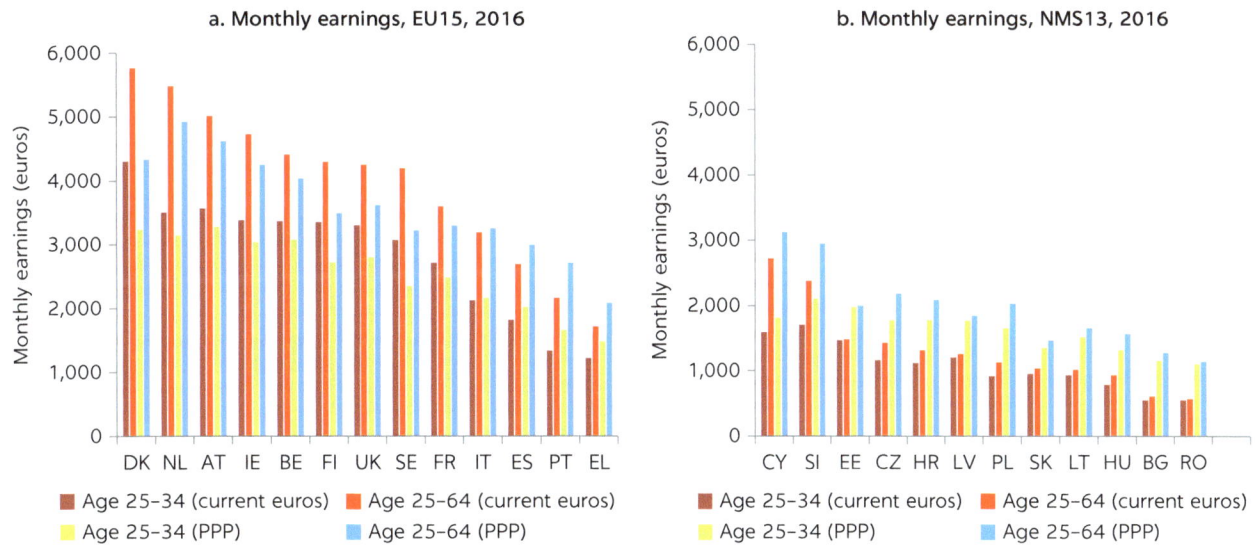

Source: World Bank elaborations based on data from Eurostat.
Note: High-skilled workers are defined as individuals with tertiary education. Wages are expressed in either current euros or euros adjusted by purchasing power standards (which takes into consideration differences in price levels). EU15 = European Union members before 2004; NMS13 = New Member States joining in 2004, 2007, and 2013; PPP = purchasing power parity.

Netherlands can expect to earn about 6.5 times the wage back home; in Denmark, the wage would be almost eight times greater (figure 1.3). Part of these large gaps is mitigated by the higher costs of living in receiving countries. Still, in purchasing power standards, young graduates from Bulgaria or Romania can expect to earn in those countries up to three times the wages in their countries of origin (third vertical bar in figure 1.3). Likewise, although a strong convergence may be observed in the share of young cohorts who have a tertiary education in the EU15 and the NMS13, the incidence of nonroutine cognitive jobs in total employment is becoming more uneven across EU regions, driven mainly by cross-country differences (figure 1.4).[6]

Social protection spending and the availability of social services also vary greatly within the EU. Important gaps persist between Western and Eastern Europe in social protection spending as a share of GDP and in per capita terms (figure 1.5). Across various categories of benefits and beneficiaries, welfare systems in Western Europe tend to be more generous in expenditures, on average, with respect to the NMS13. Expenditures on benefits related to health and sickness in the NMS13 represent 60 percent of the expenditures in the EU15. The gap becomes even greater if one considers unemployment-related welfare expenditures and last-resort antipoverty and anti–social exclusion programs. In these cases, average expenditures in the EU15, although low as a percentage of GDP, are still three times higher than the average in the NMS13. If one considers social protection expenditures in per capita terms, however, the gaps between the EU15 and the NMS13 are even more apparent. NMS13 spending is, on average, only 40 percent of the expenditures of the EU15, and the difference has been increasing. The gap in social expenditures (60 percent) is therefore even larger than the gap in income levels between the EU15 and the NMS13, which is about 40 percent.

In this context, migration flows, both internal and international, are largely a symptom rather than a cause of the socioeconomic divide and the underlying structural factors. Labor mobility can be seen as a rational response mainly to the large differentials in economic opportunities (wage gaps and job prospects) between countries and regions, and, to some extent, to the variations in the public services individuals can expect to receive, such as the quality of schooling, the quality of health care, and respect for the rule of law. On the one hand, to the

FIGURE 1.4

Tertiary educational attainment and geographic dispersion of nonroutine cognitive jobs

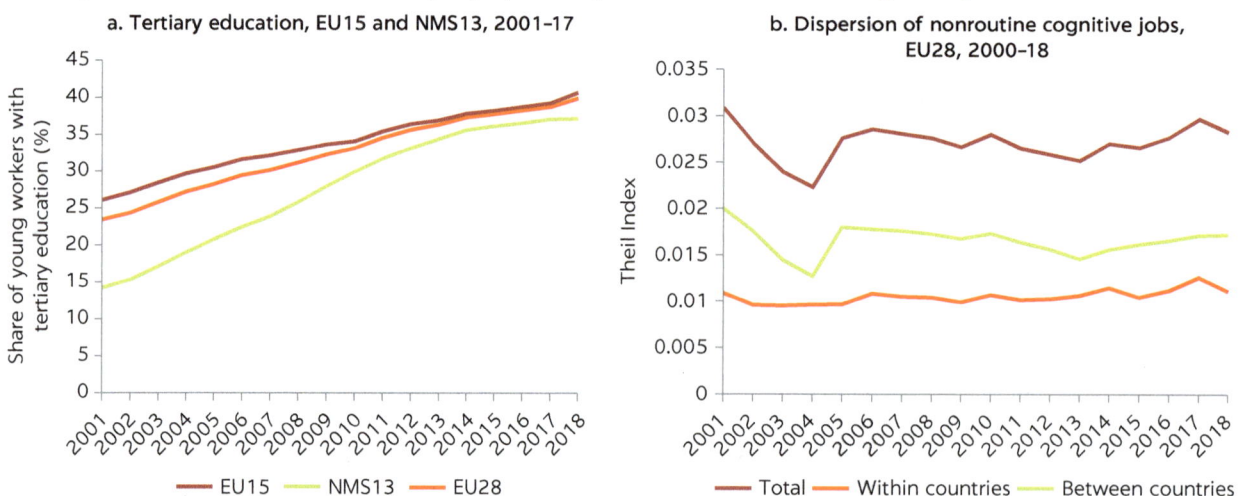

a. Tertiary education, EU15 and NMS13, 2001–17

b. Dispersion of nonroutine cognitive jobs, EU28, 2000–18

Source: World Bank elaborations based on data from Eurostat.
Note: The Theil index measures the extent of economic inequality, compared to a situation of perfect equality. A higher value of the Theil index indicates a higher level of inequality. EU15 = European Union members before 2004 (Austria, Belgium, Denmark, Finland, France, Germany, Greece, Ireland, Italy, Luxembourg, the Netherlands, Portugal, Spain, Sweden, and the United Kingdom); EU28 = EU15 + NMS13; NMS13 = New Member States joining in 2004, 2007, and 2013 (Bulgaria, Croatia, Cyprus, the Czech Republic, Estonia, Hungary, Latvia, Lithuania, Malta, Poland, Romania, the Slovak Republic, and Slovenia).

FIGURE 1.5

Differences in social protection expenditures, EU15 and NMS13

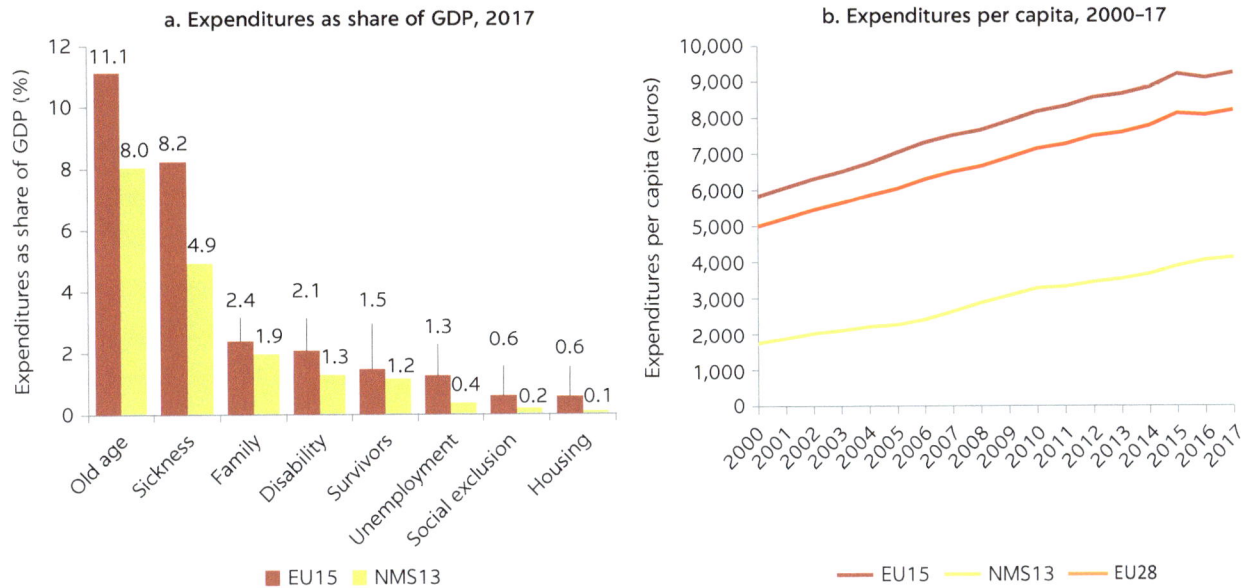

Source: World Bank elaborations based on data from Eurostat.
Note: EU15 = European Union members before 2004 (Austria, Belgium, Denmark, Finland, France, Germany, Greece, Ireland, Italy, Luxembourg, the Netherlands, Portugal, Spain, Sweden, and the United Kingdom); EU28 = EU15 + NMS13; NMS13 = New Member States joining in 2004, 2007, and 2013 (Bulgaria, Croatia, Cyprus, the Czech Republic, Estonia, Hungary, Latvia, Lithuania, Malta, Poland, Romania, the Slovak Republic, and Slovenia).

extent that migration reflects productivity differences, free movement within the EU enables workers and firms to take advantage of the potential gains in these areas. On the other hand, if migration is based on gaps in income transfers and "welfare magnets," it might even reduce efficiency. On net, economic efficiency seems to increase in both the short and the long runs as a result of migration (Clemens and Pritchett 2019). However, migration produces, a reallocation of resources that creates winners and losers among agents in sending and receiving regions, depending also on the degree of complementarity or substitutability between migrants and natives across skill groups. The next chapters provide evidence on the benefits and costs of high-skilled migration among various subgroups in both receiving and sending countries, while also distinguishing between short-term and long-term effects.

EU-wide labor mobility may contribute to greater convergence by allowing workers from lagging regions to access better opportunities across a large labor market, but it could also exacerbate geographical disparities. In the presence of free labor mobility, firms may source labor from a larger pool of workers and workers can be matched to higher-performing firms, thereby raising the efficiency of labor allocation. However, labor mobility, has also generated concerns across migrant-sending and migrant-receiving countries in the EU. Sending countries in Central, Eastern, and Southern Europe are concerned by the drain on human resources as younger, more highly skilled workers migrate for better employment opportunities in Northern and Western Europe, in the context of population aging at home. In receiving countries, the arrival of nonnative workers has raised concerns among native workers about potential adverse effects on wages and employment.

NOTES

1. The NMS13 (with year of accession) consists of the following: Cyprus, the Czech Republic, Estonia, Hungary, Latvia, Lithuania, Malta, Poland, the Slovak Republic, and Slovenia (2004); Bulgaria and Romania (2007); Croatia (2013).
2. The EU15, the full membership before 2004, consisted of Austria, Belgium, Denmark, Finland, France, Germany, Greece, Ireland, Italy, Luxembourg, the Netherlands, Portugal, Spain, Sweden, and the United Kingdom.
3. This is the population-weighted average across countries, with the EU28 representing the full EU membership before the departure of the United Kingdom in 2020 (Brexit)—that is, the EU15 plus the NMS13.
4. These results take into consideration purchasing power standards that control for differences in price levels across countries. When measuring GDP per capita in real terms (but not terms adjusted for purchasing power standards), there is also convergence across EU countries, although just three of the NMS13 (Cyprus, Malta, and Slovenia) reached higher levels in 2018 than Greece and Portugal. In comparison, in 2003, only one NMS country—Cyprus—had higher levels of GDP per capita than Greece and Portugal.
5. NUTS is a geocode classification standard for referencing subdivisions of countries for statistical purposes. In the EU, it is a hierarchical system. NUTS 2 corresponds to basic national regions and is usually composed of individual regions with populations from 800,000 to 3 million. The NUTS 2 classification has been used to determine the eligibility for aid through European Structural and Investment Funds. See "Common Classification of Territorial Units for Statistical Purposes," EUR Lex (database), Publications Office of the European Union, Luxembourg, https://eur-lex.europa.eu/legal-content/EN/TXT/?uri=LEGISSUM:g24218.
6. Nonroutine cognitive jobs include public relations and analytical, medical, and technical positions. Nonroutine activities are not repetitive or based on rules and may require flexibility and task switching. Cognitive activities involve problem solving and analysis and are associated with higher educational attainment.

REFERENCES

Clemens, Michael A., and Lant Pritchett. 2019. "The New Economic Case for Migration Restrictions: An Assessment." *Journal of Development Economics* 138: 153–64.

OECD (Organisation for Economic Co-operation and Development). 2017. "The Great Divergence(s)." OECD Science, Technology, and Innovation Policy Paper 39 (May), OECD Publishing, Paris.

Ridao-Cano, Cristobal, and Christian Bodewig. 2018. "Growing United: Upgrading Europe's Convergence Machine." World Bank Report on the European Union, World Bank, Washington, DC.

2 The Extent of Economic Migration in the European Union

Labor migration is one of the trends that has shaped the labor market of European countries, along with aging, demographic changes, and changes in the skill composition among native populations. Recent decades have been characterized by a decline in the share of youth and an increase in the share of highly skilled workers in populations in Europe and, more broadly, the Europe and Central Asia region (Docquier et al. 2018). Because workers of different ages and skill levels are typically imperfect substitutes (Card and Lemieux 2001), changes in the demographic structure have important implications for labor markets, beyond the obvious decline in the working-age population. In addition to these changes in the demographic and educational structure of the native population, the number of migrants in the European Union (EU) also nearly doubled over the period 1990–2019.[1] When compared to demographic change and progress in educational attainment, however, migration has played a more modest role in the employment and wage dynamics of native workers in recent decades (Docquier et al. 2018).

INCREASED MIGRATION IN THE EU SINCE 1990

The European economic landscape has undergone an impressive transformation since the early 1990s through global economic integration and international migration. The stock of economic migrants in the EU has more than doubled over the past 30 years. The total number of foreign-born residents in EU countries (either from EU or non-EU Member States) reached 60 million in 2019. This number represents 12 percent of the EU resident population and over 23 percent of the stock of global migrants, whereas the EU population accounts for only 6.7 percent of the total world population.

Among the current stock of the foreign born in EU countries, more than 21 million individuals, or 35 percent of the total, are migrants from other EU member countries (figure 2.1). Of these intra-EU migrants, 11 million (18 percent) have arrived from the EU15.[2] Another 10 million (17 percent), up from 4 million in 2000, have come from the 13 New Member States (the NMS13) joining the EU in 2004, 2007, and 2013.[3] An additional 10 million

FIGURE 2.1

The foreign-born population in the European Union, 1990–2019

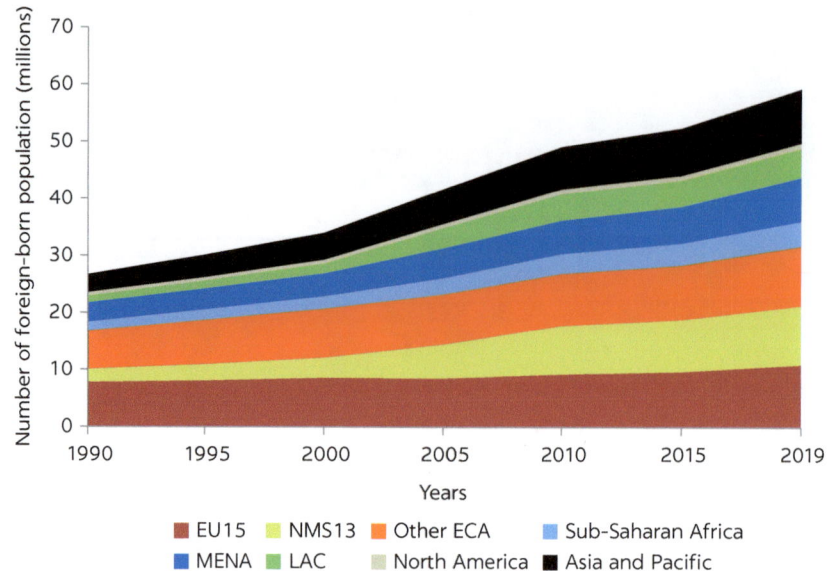

Source: International Migration (database), Population Division, Department of Economic and Social Affairs, United Nations, https://www.un.org/en/development/desa/population /migration/data/index.asp.
Note: ECA = Europe and Central Asia; EU15 = European Union members before 2004 (Austria, Belgium, Denmark, Finland, France, Germany, Greece, Ireland, Italy, Luxembourg, the Netherlands, Portugal, Spain, Sweden, and the United Kingdom); LAC = Latin America and the Caribbean; MENA = Middle East and North Africa; NMS13 = New Member States joining in 2004, 2007, and 2013 (Bulgaria, Croatia, Cyprus, the Czech Republic, Estonia, Hungary, Latvia, Lithuania, Malta, Poland, Romania, the Slovak Republic, and Slovenia).

(17 percent) are migrants from non-EU European countries in the western Balkans, Turkey, Eastern Europe, and the European Free Trade Association (EFTA).[4] The remaining 28 million migrants (more than 46 percent) come from other regions of the world.

Immigration is uneven across the EU and is largely concentrated in the EU15. More than 90 percent of all immigrants to the EU reside in the EU15. Also, in per capita terms, a higher relative share of immigrants resides in the EU15 (figure 2.2). Luxemburg has the largest relative share of the foreign born in the total population, at 50 percent. In Austria, Belgium, Cyprus, Germany, Ireland, Malta, and Sweden, the share of immigrants in the population varies between 15 percent and 20 percent. Immigration is also increasing from low starting levels in several of the NMS13, although in many cases this new phenomenon is significantly underreported. Box 2.1 discusses the role of Poland as an emerging immigration country and the difficulties of providing accurate estimates. By region of origin, EU nationals represent the majority of immigrants in only a few smaller countries (Cyprus, Hungary, Ireland, Luxemburg, Malta, and the Slovak Republic). Nonetheless, the share of EU immigrants among all foreign residents in Austria, Belgium, Germany, and the United Kingdom is sizable, ranging between 39 percent and 46 percent.

Labor mobility within the EU is relatively low by international standards. Only a small share of the total EU28 population is mobile across internal EU borders.[5] Labor mobility is much lower in the EU28 than between the Australian

FIGURE 2.2

Foreign-born residents in the total European Union population, January 2019

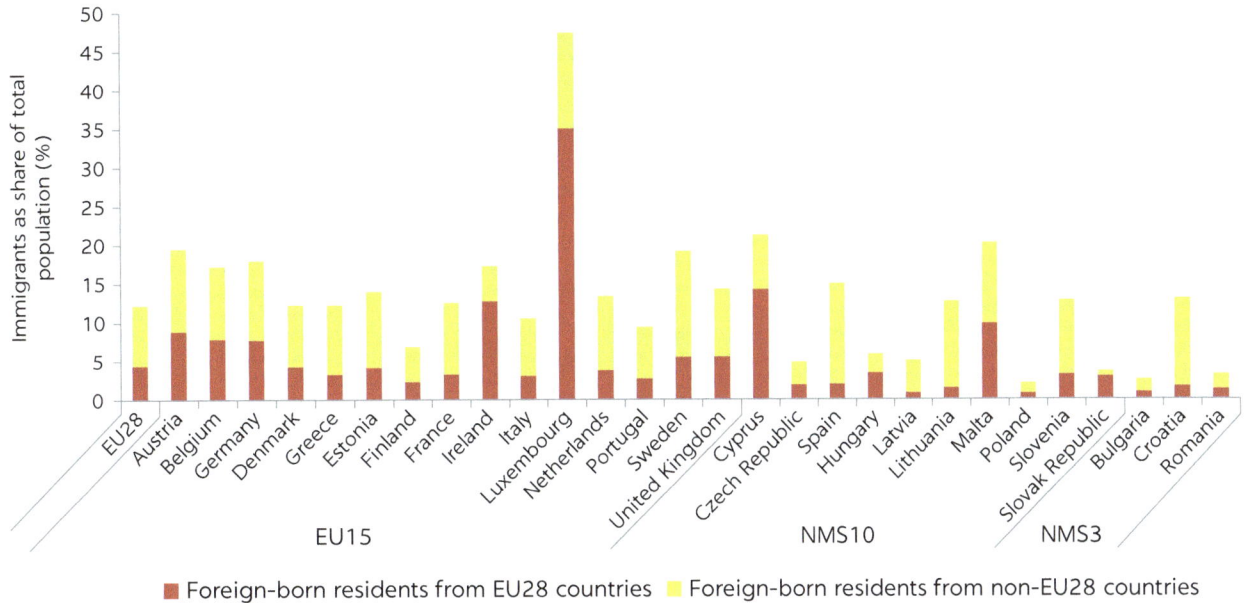

Source: International Migration (database), Population Division, Department of Economic and Social Affairs, United Nations, https://www.un.org/en/development/desa/population/migration/data/index.asp.
Note: EU15 = European Union members before 2004; EU28 = EU15 + NMS; NMS10 = New Member States that completed formal EU accession in 2004; NMS3 = New Member States that completed formal EU accession in 2007 (Bulgaria and Romania) or 2013 (Croatia).

Box 2.1

The duality of Poland as a high-emigration and -immigration country

Poland has a long tradition of emigration, mostly to Western Europe and North America. Since joining the European Union (EU) in 2004, Poland has seen emigration increase sharply, raising the stock of Polish abroad from about 1.8 million in 2003 to 4.0 million in 2018 (figure B2.1.1, panel a). These trends have put Poland at the top of migrant-sending countries in the EU. The main increases in the Polish diaspora were in the United Kingdom (from 34,000 in 2003 to close to 1 million in 2016, although it has declined since then) and Germany (from 0.7 million in 2003 to more than 1.6 million in 2018).

At the root of these migration flows are the lifting of entry restrictions for EU countries and the sizable gaps in earnings, social services, and other amenities. Polish emigrants tend to be younger and more educated than the general population of the country. According to census statistics compiled by the

Organisation for Economic Co-operation and Development (OECD) Database on Immigrants in OECD and non-OECD Countries (DIOC), about 36 percent of adult Polish emigrants had a tertiary education in 2010–11, compared to 23 percent of the population in Poland. The selection of emigrants in age and education has exacerbated the reduction of the labor force and shortages in specific occupations requiring low or high skills. Job vacancies rose to 125,400 jobs in 2019 (representing 1 percent of total employment), mostly in low-skill occupations in manufacturing and construction, but also in high-skill professional occupations in the information and communication technology, research, and health care sectors (Statistics Poland 2020a).

The increasing number of job vacancies and large wage differentials with neighboring non-EU Eastern European countries have fueled a newer

continued

Box 2.1, *continued*

Emigration and immigration in Poland

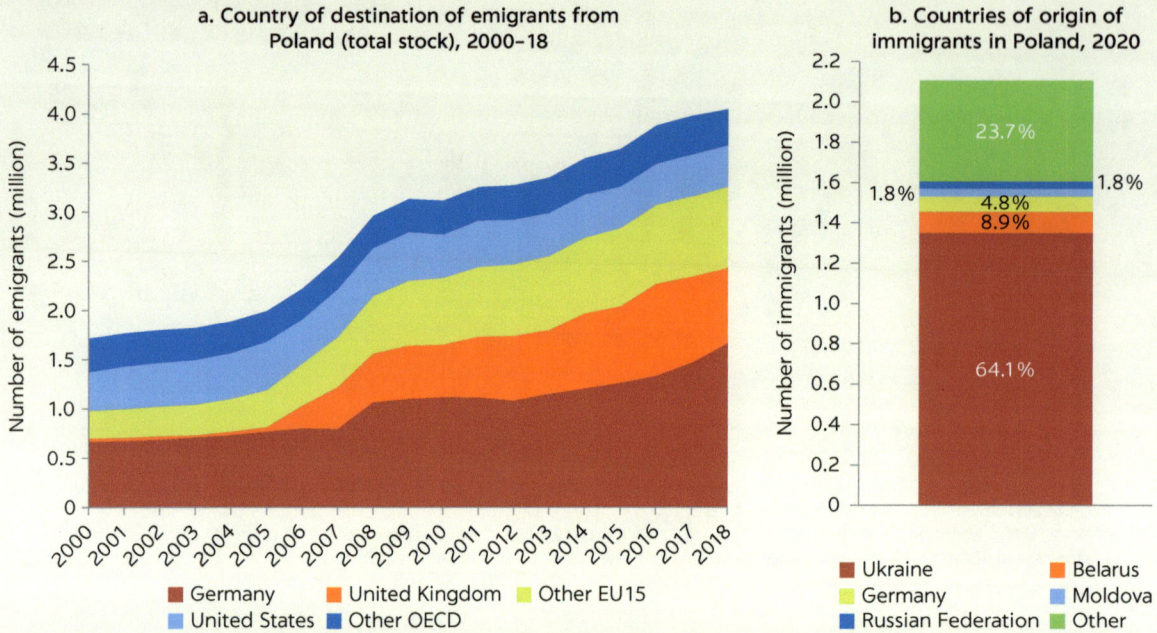

a. Country of destination of emigrants from Poland (total stock), 2000–18

b. Countries of origin of immigrants in Poland, 2020

Sources: Annual stock of Polish emigrants: International Migration Database, Organisation for Economic Co-operation and Development, https://stats.oecd.org/Index.aspx?DataSetCode=MIG. Share of immigrants in Poland: Statistics Poland (2020b).
Note: EU15 = European Union members before 2004 (Austria, Belgium, Denmark, Finland, France, Germany, Greece, Ireland, Italy, Luxembourg, the Netherlands, Portugal, Spain, Sweden, and the United Kingdom); OECD = Organisation for Economic Co-operation and Development.

immigration phenomenon. Despite a long history of immigration in Poland from former Soviet Union countries, inflows of foreigners have increased sharply, turning Poland into a net recipient of migration since 2016. Official statistics of foreigners with work permits rose from 65,000 in 2015 to 445,000 in 2019. However, given Poland's labor shortages, since 2006 it has allowed workers from Belarus, the Russian Federation, and Ukraine to work in Poland without work permits on the basis of employers' declarations (not contracts) of intent to employ them for up to six months within one year. Most such declarations come from agriculture and construction, which have higher demand for seasonal workers. This policy has promoted temporary and circular migration with neighboring non-EU Eastern European countries.

The temporary nature of immigration in the country has created challenges in estimating the true size of the immigrant population. Statistics Poland (2020b) estimates that, in 2019, Poland had 2.1 million immigrants (5.5 percent of the country's population). About two-thirds of migrants (1.35 million) came from Ukraine alone, and 105,000 came from Belarus (figure B2.1.1, panel b). Eurostat data also show that, of EU countries, Poland issued the most first-time residence permits to non-EU immigrants in 2017 and 2018. According to recent surveys targeted to immigrants, their profile is of a younger population with lower education qualifications and a sizable occupational downgrade; many temporary migrants work in low-skill jobs (National Bank of Poland 2019).

The Polish government has repeatedly expressed its priority to attract Polish migrants back to fill shortages of labor and to balance the aging population. According to the EU Labour Force Survey, of the 3.1 million Polish living abroad in 2010, 1.7 million had

continued

Box 2.1, *continued*

already returned home in 2014. However, two main challenges remain. First, Poland's labor shortages might be larger than the current size of the Polish diaspora. Poland's Union of Entrepreneurs and Employers (2018) estimates that the country will need 5 million new workers by 2050 in order to maintain the pace of economic growth. Thus, migration policy should promote the return of emigrants and immigration flows from other countries. Second, the lower education levels of immigrants compared to the Polish remaining in Poland and of Polish returnees compared to emigrants staying abroad highlight the additional challenge the country faces in attracting talent and workers with higher skills.

or US states. Intra-EU mobility is similar to the mobility between Quebec and other provinces of Canada; that is, it is similar to situations in which language barriers apply (Ridao-Cano and Bodewig 2018). Therefore, the potential of the free-movement area of the EU to serve as a major adjustment channel for labor reallocation may be underexploited.

RAPID RISE IN EMIGRATION FROM EASTERN EUROPE AFTER THE EU EXPANSION

From the perspective of the countries of origin, the rise in emigration from the NMS13 countries since EU accession has been rapid. The EU enlargement and the resulting greater freedom of movement have facilitated labor migration across countries, in particular from the NMS13 to Western Europe. As figure 2.3 shows, emigration rates ranged from 14 percent to 17 percent in Bulgaria, Croatia, Lithuania, and Romania in 2018 (see box 2.2 for a more detailed description of migration trends in Croatia). In Latvia and Poland, the share of emigrants in the population stands at about 10 percent. The NMS13 countries with relatively higher income have experienced the lowest emigration rates, which is the case for the Czech Republic, Hungary, and Slovenia. Emigration rates are generally lower in Western Europe, at an average of about 5 percent, with the exceptions of Ireland (20 percent) and Portugal (15 percent).

Most NMS13 emigrants migrate to the EU15, whereas EU15 emigrants remain within the EU15 or emigrate to the rest of the world. Overall, there are 22.7 million emigrants from the EU15 and 14.1 million emigrants from the NMS13 countries (figure 2.4). By region of destination, NMS13 emigrants are highly concentrated in the EU15 (69 percent). Other main destinations include non-EU European countries (10 percent) and non-European countries, mostly advanced economies of the Organisation for Economic Co-operation and Development (OECD) (13 percent). EU15 emigrants are more dispersed across the globe. Among them, 45 percent are in other EU15 countries, and the remaining 41 percent are mostly in non-European OECD countries, such as Australia, Canada, and the United States. Another 7 percent reside in the EFTA countries.

FIGURE 2.3

Share of emigrants in the native population, European Union countries, 2001, 2009, and 2018

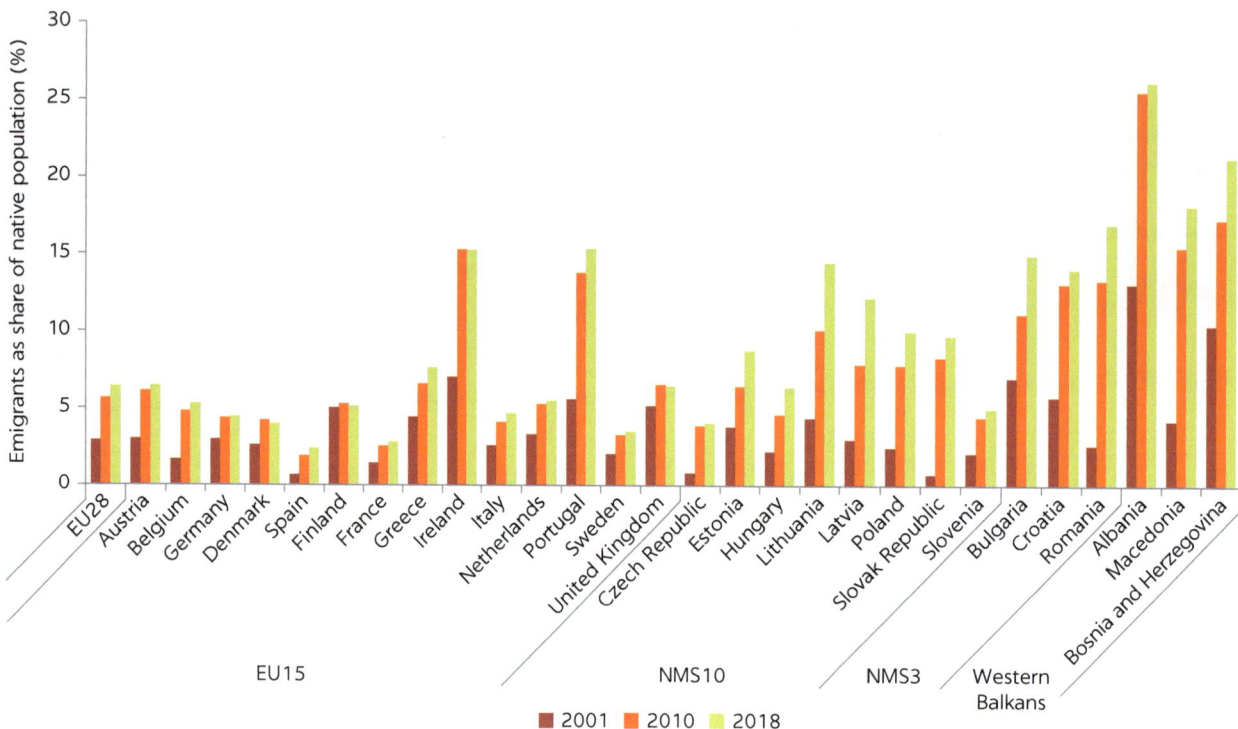

Sources: Stock of emigrants: International Migration Database, OECD Statistics, Organisation for Economic Co-operation and Development, https://stats.oecd.org/Index.aspx?DataSetCode=MIG. Population: World Population Prospects 2019 (database), Population Division, Department of Economic and Social Affairs, United Nations, https://population.un.org/wpp/.
Note: The emigration rate is the total number of emigrants, divided by the size of the native population in the country of origin or abroad. EU15 = European Union members before 2004; EU28 = EU15 + NMS; NMS10 = New Member States that completed formal EU accession in 2004; NMS3 = New Member States that completed formal EU accession in 2007 (Bulgaria and Romania) or 2013 (Croatia).

Box 2.2

The changing nature of emigration flows in Croatia

Croatia has seen an increase in emigration since its European Union (EU) accession in 2013. According to the Croatian Bureau of Statistics, the flows of emigrants, which averaged fewer than 10,000 per year between 2000 and 2012, rapidly increased to a peak of 47,000 in 2017, averaging close to 33,000 annually between 2013 and 2019 (figure B2.2.1, panel a). However, official estimates tend to underreport the emigration phenomenon because they are based on self-reporting by emigrants who have little incentives to do so, given that the process is bureaucratic and brings about the loss of domestic social security benefits. Draženović, Kunovac, and Pripužić (2018), using data from national statistical offices of EU destination countries to approximate the size of migration flows coming from Croatia,

find that between 2013 and 2016, 230,000 people left Croatia to core EU countries (a number 2.6 times higher than official Croatian statistics).

Recent estimates by the United Nations Department of Economic and Social Affairs population division put the total stock of Croatians living abroad at about 1 million. During the 1990s, the war in the Balkans caused the forced displacement of about one-fifth of the population, mostly internally or in neighboring countries, although 150,000 people from Croatia moved to Western European countries (Župarić-Iljć and Bara 2014). Most recent emigration flows have been concentrated in Western EU countries. Since EU accession, about half of Croatian emigrants have moved to Germany, 7 percent to Austria,

continued

Box 2.2, *continued*

FIGURE B2.2.1

Immigration and emigration trends and age composition of emigrants, Croatia

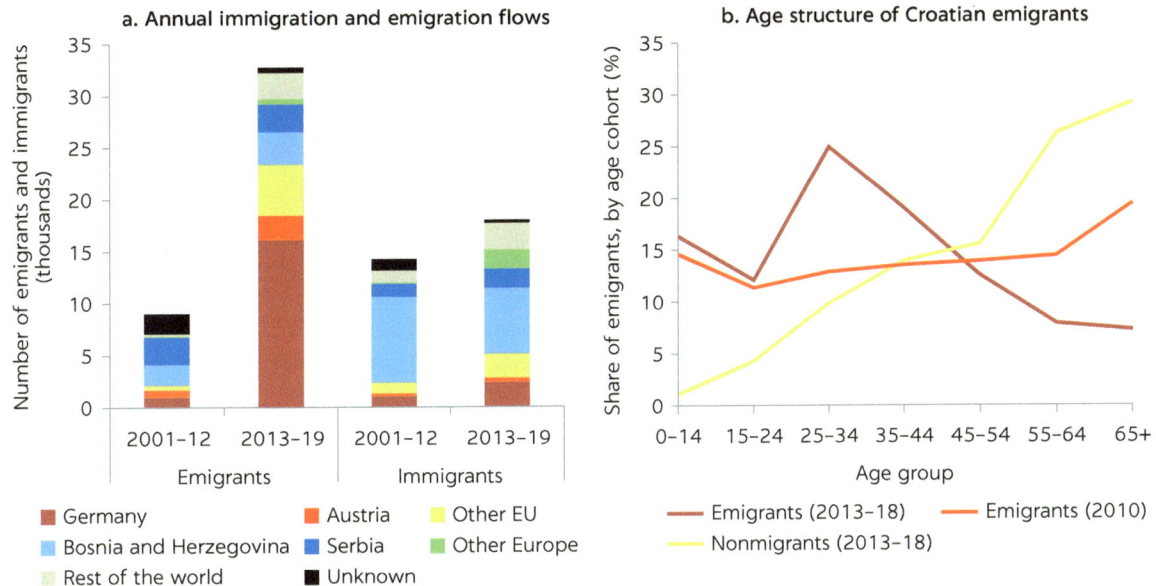

Sources: Immigration and emigration flows: Immigrant and emigrant population to/from Croatia, Croatian Bureau of Statistics, https://www.dzs.hr/default_e.htm. Demographic profile of emigrants (2013–18): Emigration (database), Eurostat, European Commission, reference years 2013/18, Emigration by age group, sex, and country of birth [migr_emi4ctb], https://ec.europa.eu/eurostat/en/web/products-datasets/-/MIGR_EMI4CTB. Demographic profile of emigrants in 2010: DIOC (Database on Immigrants in OECD and Non-OECD Countries), reference years 2010/11, Organisation for Economic Co-operation and Development, https://www.oecd.org/els/mig/dioc.htm. Demographic profile of nonmigrants: Population (database), Eurostat, European Commission, reference years 2013/18, Population on January 1, by age group and sex [demo_pjangroup], https://ec.europa.eu/eurostat/web/population/overview. *Note:* EU = European Union.

and 15 percent to other EU countries (figure B2.2.1, panel a). Another 18 percent of emigrants went to neighboring Bosnia and Herzegovina and Serbia, although some are Bosnian and Serbian nationals returning to their home countries.

The sociodemographic composition of Croatian emigrants has evolved in recent years. Up to 2010, men represented 46.7 percent of total emigrants, but, since EU accession, their share has increased to 53.0 percent. Recent emigration flows present a high incidence of young and prime-age groups; emigrants between 15 and 44 years of age account for 56 percent of total migrants, compared to only 28 percent in 2010 (figure B2.2.1, panel b). Economic migrants tend to be younger than forcibly displaced populations (Cortes 2004), and much of the latter group stay abroad for a longer time or never return.

Different studies show that EU accession has been at the forefront of determinants of the acceleration in

migration outflows (Draženović, Kunovac, and Pripužić 2018; Župarić-Iljć 2016). Entry into the single market and subsequent freedom of movement have allowed many Croatians to take advantage of the large income differentials with EU15 countries. Further economic factors—such as the global financial crisis, which severely hit the Croatian economy—and high youth unemployment—which at 50 percent in 2013 was third-highest in the EU—have fueled emigration flows (Župarić-Iljć 2016), particularly of youth. In a survey of Croatians in Germany, Jurić (2017) finds that noneconomic factors have also had an important role in emigration decisions. Among them, demographics and the prevalence of corruption in the country are frequently cited (Draženović, Kunovac, and Pripužić 2018).

Limited data availability makes it difficult to analyze the educational profile of emigrants. Statistics from census data of Organisation for Economic Co-operation and Development destination countries

continued

Box 2.2, *continued*

in 2010 suggest that the educational profile of emigrants was broadly neutral vis-à-vis nonmigrants, with 17 percent having tertiary education—compared to 16 percent of nonmigrants. However, more recent emigrants after EU accession seem to have slightly lower education levels, with a larger increase in outflows among low-educated workers (Župarić-Iljić 2016). Still, the emigration of qualified professionals—particularly health workers—has been highlighted as a potential concern (Gruber et al. 2020). Between 2013 and 2018, a yearly average of 136 doctors and 289 nurses emigrated to other EU countries, a drain of 1 percent of the stock of doctors per year.[a] However, these outflows have been compensated by a more rapid increase in new cohorts of medical doctors, lifting the stock in the country from 299 per 100,000 inhabitants in 2012 to 344 in 2018.

Migration from Croatia provides opportunities for emigrants and the country, easing unemployment pressures and strengthening social and economic networks and knowledge transfer. At the same time, emigration of young Croatians creates challenges for the country's demographic structure, human capital, and labor market. To curb some of the outflows, the government is starting to address some of the push factors. For example, unemployed young entrepreneurs can apply for subsidies of up to 130,000 Croatian kunas (about 17,000 euros) to be allocated from EU funds. However, given the large income differentials in the EU, it is difficult to successfully attract emigrants back to the country. In 2014, there were only 78,000 returnees in Croatia,[b] less than 10 percent of the stock of emigrants in 2010 and giving Croatia the lowest returnee rate in Europe.

a. Based on data from the Regulated Professions Database, European Commission, https://ec.europa.eu/growth/tools-databases/regprof/.
b. Based on data from the EU Labour Force Survey ad hoc migration module.

FIGURE 2.4

Share of emigrants from the European Union, by region of origin and destination, 2019

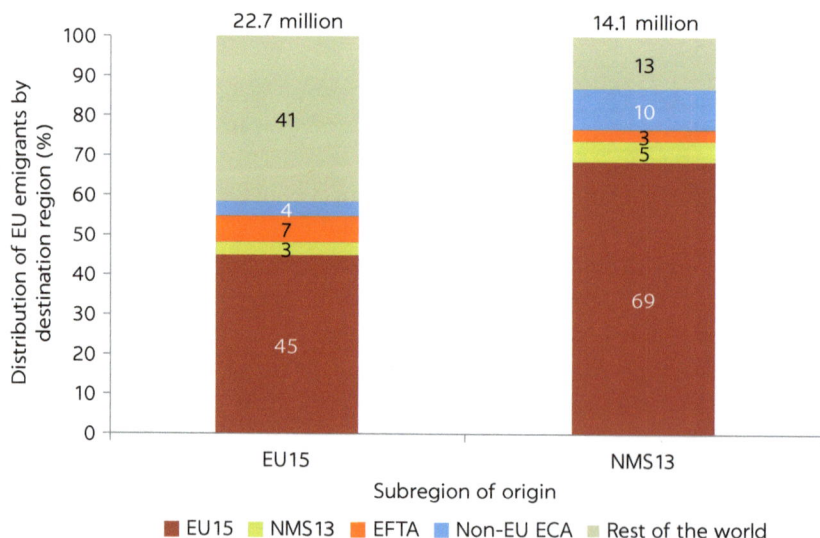

Source: International Migration (database), Population Division, Department of Economic and Social Affairs, United Nations, https://www.un.org/en/development/desa/population/migration/data/index.asp.
Note: ECA = Europe and Central Asia (Non-EU ECA countries include: Albania, Armenia, Azerbaijan, Belarus, Bosnia and Herzegovina, Georgia, Kazakhstan, Kyrgyzstan, Montenegro, North Macedonia, Republic of Moldova, Russia, Serbia, Tajikistan, Turkey, Turkmenistan, Ukraine, and Uzbekistan); EFTA = Andorra, Channel Islands, Faroe Islands, Gibraltar, Greenland, Holy See, Iceland, Isle of Man, Liechtenstein, Monaco, Norway, San Marino, and Switzerland. EU15 = European Union members before 2004 (Austria, Belgium, Denmark, Finland, France, Germany, Greece, Ireland, Italy, Luxembourg, the Netherlands, Portugal, Spain, Sweden, and the United Kingdom); NMS13 = New Member States joining in 2004, 2007, and 2013 (Bulgaria, Croatia, Cyprus, the Czech Republic, Estonia, Hungary, Latvia, Lithuania, Malta, Poland, Romania, the Slovak Republic, and Slovenia).

THE (EVEN FASTER) INCREASE IN SKILLED MIGRATION IN THE EU IN THE PAST 15 YEARS

Skilled migration to the EU has risen even more rapidly than overall migration over the past 15 years. The number of high-skilled migrants in the EU, defined as migrants with some tertiary education, more than tripled over the period 2004–18, increasing from about 4 million to 13 million. The rise in high-skilled migration has been largely driven by migrants from outside the EU, whose numbers rose from 2.8 million in 2004 to 8.3 million in 2018. Although smaller in absolute numbers, intra-EU15 high-skilled migration increased by a factor of seven over the same period, from 0.3 million in 2004 to 2.1 million in 2018. Meanwhile, high-skilled migration from the NMS13 rose at a more modest pace, from 1.2 million to 2.7 million. The total intra-EU28 mobility of high-skilled workers has increased faster than total migration (European Commission 2021). Like overall migration, the concentration of highly educated migrants is largely in EU15 countries (97 percent of all skilled migrants in the EU28).

In relative terms, the skill content of migration to the EU28 also increased, especially for internal migration within the EU15. Migrants from EU15 countries in other EU countries have traditionally had higher educational attainment relative to the overall population of the EU15. This pattern has become more pronounced over time, as the share of migrants with tertiary education from the EU15 has risen more rapidly than the corresponding share in the overall population in the EU (figure 2.5). In recent years, almost half the migrants from the EU15 in other EU countries had tertiary degrees. Compared to migrants from the EU15, migrants from the NMS13 have lower overall educational attainment, reflecting the lower human capital in origin countries. In addition, the share of migrants with tertiary education has increased less

FIGURE 2.5

Tertiary education, age 25–64, natives and foreign-born, European Union

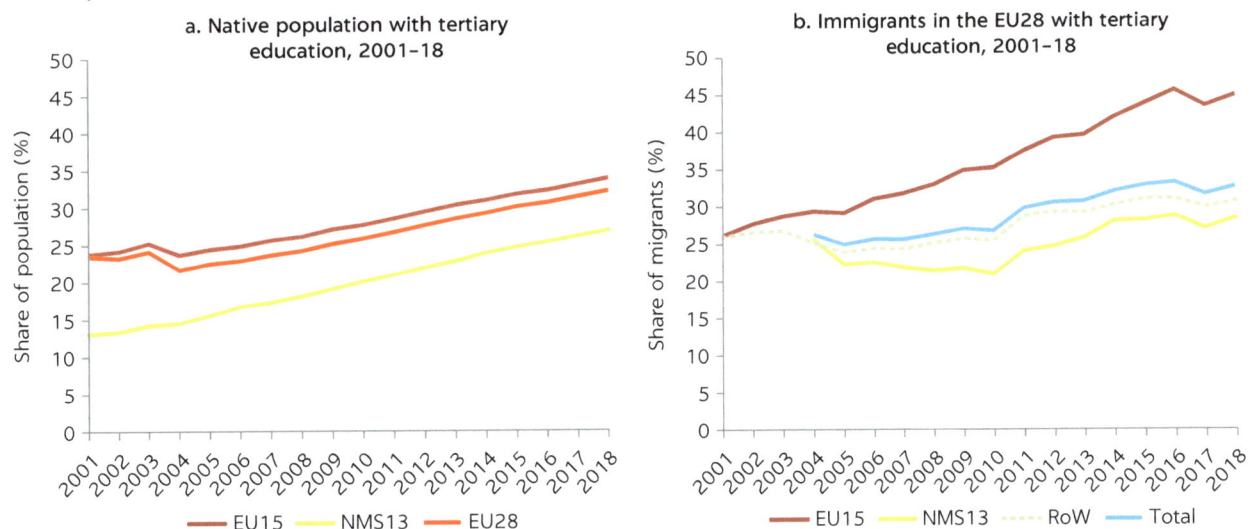

Source: Estimates based on data from the European Union Labour Force Survey (database), Eurostat, European Commission, https://ec.europa.eu/eurostat /statistics-explained/index.php/EU_labour_force_survey.
Note: EU15 = European Union members before 2004 (Austria, Belgium, Denmark, Finland, France, Germany, Greece, Ireland, Italy, Luxembourg, the Netherlands, Portugal, Spain, Sweden, and the United Kingdom); EU28 = EU15 + NMS13; NMS13 = New Member States joining in 2004, 2007, and 2013 (Bulgaria, Croatia, Cyprus, the Czech Republic, Estonia, Hungary, Latvia, Lithuania, Malta, Poland, Romania, the Slovak Republic, and Slovenia); RoW = rest of the world.

rapidly among migrants from the NMS13 and from the rest of the world than among migrants from the EU15.

In line with the upward trends in education, the share of individuals in occupations that require nonroutine tasks has risen more quickly among migrants than among the overall EU population. Reflecting technological change, the share of workers engaged in nonroutine cognitive tasks in the EU has been increasing, although at a moderate pace. The share has been growing more rapidly in the EU15 than in the NMS13 (figure 2.6). Meanwhile, the share of individuals engaged in such activities has risen more quickly among migrants from the EU15 than among the overall EU population, reflecting the large increase in the share of high-skilled migrants from the EU15. In addition, the share of migrants from the NMS13 and the rest of the world engaged in nonroutine cognitive tasks has risen at a more moderate pace, although still more rapidly relative to the share among the overall population.

The skill composition of migration greatly differs across destination countries in the EU. Reflecting geographical disparities in productivity, skill shortages, and skill-specific wage premiums across the EU, high-skilled migrants are disproportionately concentrated in certain countries and in certain regions within countries in Europe (map 2.1, panel a). In most regions of the Nordic countries and the United Kingdom, for example, more than half of the migrants from the EU are equipped with tertiary education. In Italy, in contrast, a minority of migrants have attained some tertiary education. In countries such as France and Spain, the prevalence of highly skilled migrants varies quite substantially by region. In terms of the share of the total adult population (age 25–64), high-skilled migrants represent more than 15 percent in some urban areas in Ireland, Switzerland, and the southeastern United Kingdom, which surpasses the 10 percent in the metropolitan areas of Luxembourg, Paris, Stockholm, and

FIGURE 2.6

Workers age 25–64 employed in nonroutine cognitive jobs, European Union

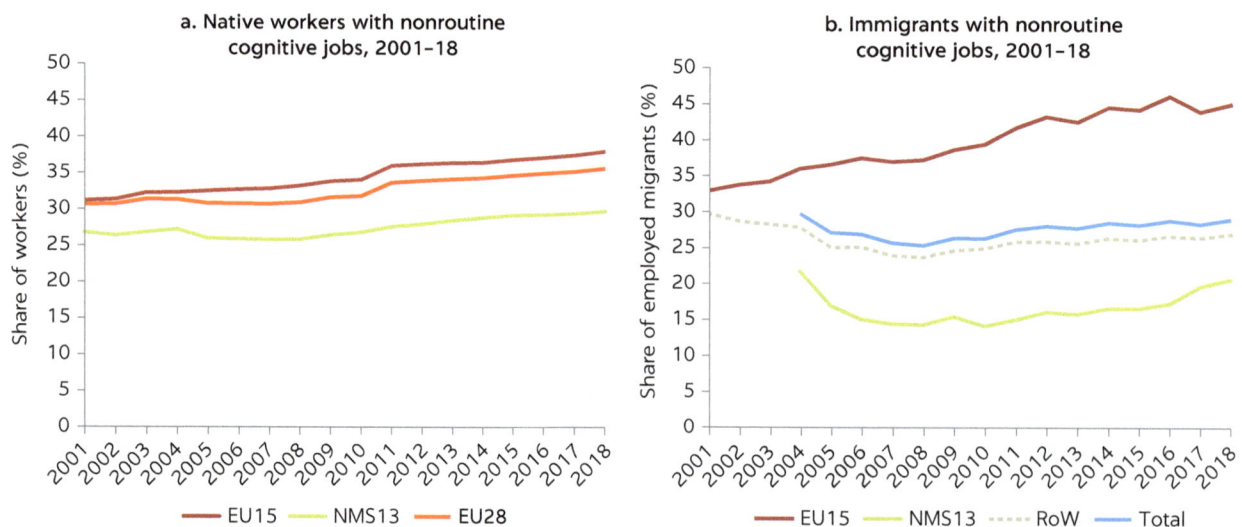

Source: Estimates based on data from the European Union Labour Force Survey (database), Eurostat, European Commission, https://ec.europa.eu/eurostat/statistics-explained/index.php/EU_labour_force_survey.
Note: EU15 = European Union members before 2004 (Austria, Belgium, Denmark, Finland, France, Germany, Greece, Ireland, Italy, Luxembourg, the Netherlands, Portugal, Spain, Sweden, and the United Kingdom); EU28 = EU15 + NMS13; NMS13 = New Member States joining in 2004, 2007, and 2013 (Bulgaria, Croatia, Cyprus, the Czech Republic, Estonia, Hungary, Latvia, Lithuania, Malta, Poland, Romania, the Slovak Republic, and Slovenia); RoW = rest of the world.

MAP 2.1

Educational attainment of immigrants, European Union regions

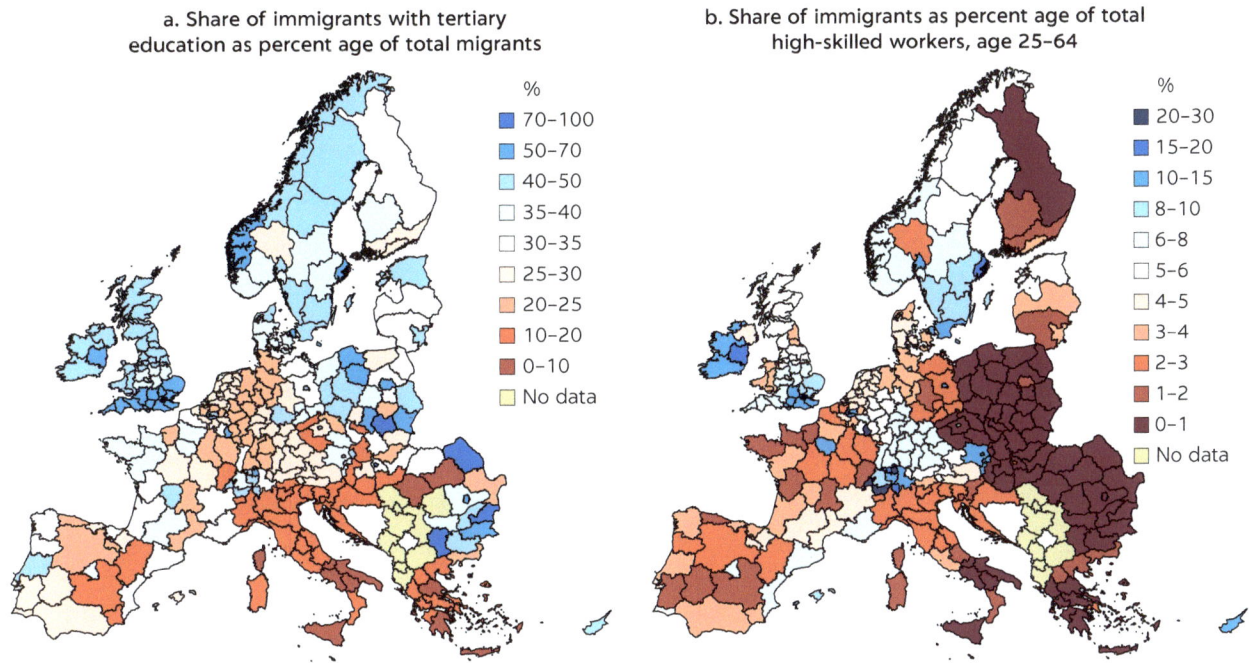

a. Share of immigrants with tertiary
education as percent age of total migrants

b. Share of immigrants as percent age of total
high-skilled workers, age 25–64

%
- 70–100
- 50–70
- 40–50
- 35–40
- 30–35
- 25–30
- 20–25
- 10–20
- 0–10
- No data

%
- 20–30
- 15–20
- 10–15
- 8–10
- 6–8
- 5–6
- 4–5
- 3–4
- 2–3
- 1–2
- 0–1
- No data

Source: Estimates based on data from the European Union Labour Force Survey (database), Eurostat, European Commission, https://ec.europa.eu/eurostat /statistics-explained/index.php/EU_labour_force_survey.

Vienna. In contrast, Italian regions, despite receiving a large share of migrants overall, host relatively few high-skilled migrants.

CHARACTERISTICS OF HIGH-SKILLED MIGRANTS IN THE EU

In contrast to the broad gender parity among migrants from the EU15, women are overrepresented among migrants from the NMS13, especially among the highly educated. In addition, the share of women among NMS13 migrants with tertiary education has been rising, whereas it has remained fairly constant among migrants from the EU15 (figure 2.7). Women also used to be overrepresented among low-educated migrants from the NMS13; the share of women, although declining, is still greater than the share of men. For migrants with intermediate levels of schooling, there is close to gender party, although the share of females is again slightly higher among migrants from the NMS13.

Highly educated migrants are more concentrated among younger age groups and, although filling key gaps in the labor market, they suffer from occupational downgrade. High-skilled migrants, like all migrants, tend to be clustered in the 25–44 age group (figure 2.8, panel a). This is particularly true for high-skilled migrants coming from NMS13 countries, among whom 70 percent are within that age range, compared to 54 percent of natives. In contrast, high-skilled migrants from EU15 countries have an age distribution more similar that of natives. A key characteristic of many high-skilled migrants in host labor markets is overqualification and occupational downgrade (Aleksynska and Tritah 2013). On average, migrants with tertiary education have 2.5 more years of education

FIGURE 2.7

Share of women among migrants, by education level, European Union, 2001–17

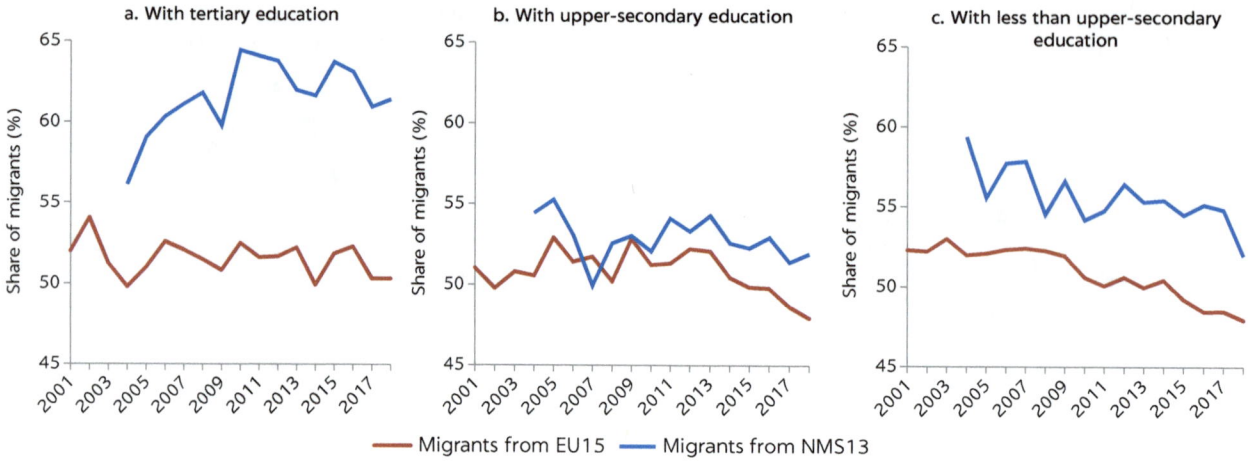

a. With tertiary education

b. With upper-secondary education

c. With less than upper-secondary education

Migrants from EU15   Migrants from NMS13

Source: Estimates based on data from the European Union Labour Force Survey (database), Eurostat, European Commission, https://ec.europa.eu/eurostat /statistics-explained/index.php/EU_labour_force_survey.

Note: EU15 = European Union members before 2004 (Austria, Belgium, Denmark, Finland, France, Germany, Greece, Ireland, Italy, Luxembourg, the Netherlands, Portugal, Spain, Sweden, and the United Kingdom); NMS13 = New Member States joining in 2004, 2007, and 2013 (Bulgaria, Croatia, Cyprus, the Czech Republic, Estonia, Hungary, Latvia, Lithuania, Malta, Poland, Romania, the Slovak Republic, and Slovenia).

FIGURE 2.8

Demographic and occupational distribution of tertiary-educated immigrants relative to natives, European Union, 2018

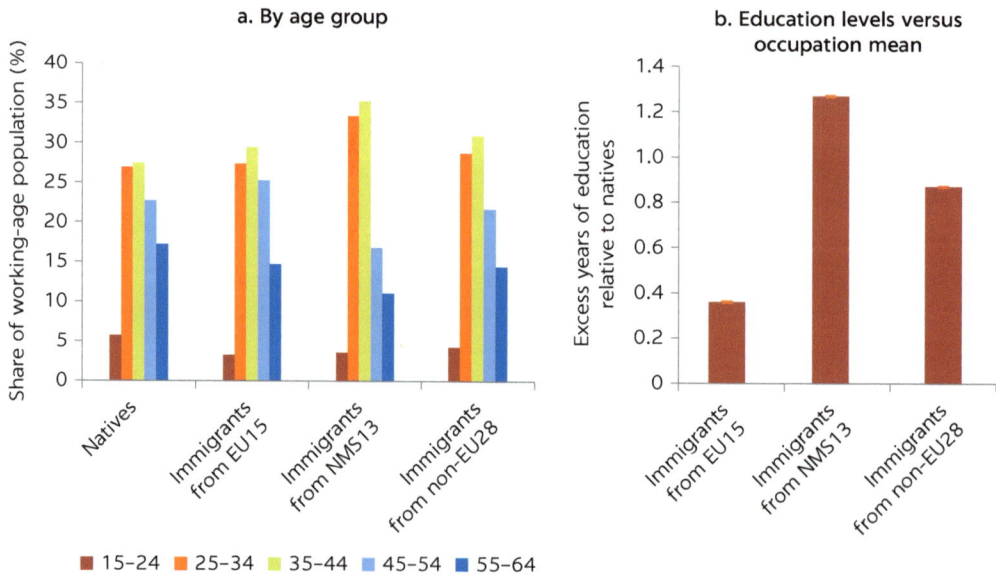

a. By age group

b. Education levels versus occupation mean

15–24   25–34   35–44   45–54   55–64

Source: Estimates based on data from the European Union Labour Force Survey (database).

Note: Panel b compares the excess education of tertiary-educated migrants versus tertiary-educated natives. Excess education refers to a person's number of years of education compared to the average years of education of workers in the same occupation (using ISCO-08 three-digit level). EU15 = European Union members before 2004 (Austria, Belgium, Denmark, Finland, France, Germany, Greece, Ireland, Italy, Luxembourg, the Netherlands, Portugal, Spain, Sweden, and the United Kingdom); EU28 = EU15 + NMS13; ISCO = International Standard Classification of Occupations; NMS13 = New Member States joining in 2004, 2007, and 2013 (Bulgaria, Croatia, Cyprus, the Czech Republic, Estonia, Hungary, Latvia, Lithuania, Malta, Poland, Romania, the Slovak Republic, and Slovenia).

than the average worker in their same occupation, measured at the ISCO-08 three-digit level,[6] whereas high-skilled natives have 1.7 additional years of schooling. That is, overqualification of highly educated migrants is 46 percent higher than that of similarly educated natives.

By region of origin, occupational downgrade particularly affects highly educated migrants from the NMS13. Immigrants from the NMS13 have on average 1.3 more years of schooling than natives in the same occupation, whereas the gap is only 0.3 year for tertiary-educated EU15 migrants (figure 2.8, panel b). According to the 2018 EU Labour Force Survey, 5 out of the top 10 occupations in which highly educated male NMS13 migrants work can be categorized as low-skill occupations (building frame workers, heavy truck/bus drivers, building finishers, transportation/storage workers, and machinery mechanics) compared to none of the top 10 occupations for high-skilled male natives (figure 2.9, panels a and b). Female workers have a different occupational profile than males, as has been shown in past regional studies (for example, Munoz Boudet et al. 2021). However, similar patterns of occupational downgrade emerge for qualified NMS13 female migrant workers—5 of the top 10 jobs require medium to low skill levels (figure 2.9, panel d).

Migrants also self-select into occupations that have a different task content than natives' occupations. Even without occupational downgrade, NMS13 migrants tend to work in different occupations from natives, because natives are more likely to have jobs that require more communication skills (for example, sales, legal and finance professionals, teachers, and administrative workers), whereas high-skilled migrants select occupations that require more quantitative or analytical skills, such as information and communication technology (ICT) software developers, engineers, and medical doctors (figure 2.9). The occupational downgrade of migrants upon arrival in the host country has been linked to the lack of local specific skills, including language skills and the imperfect recognition of human capital obtained abroad (Borjas 2015; Friedberg 2000). Therefore, the occupational clustering of highly educated migrants also shows the selection into tasks for which they have a comparative advantage (Peri and Sparber 2011).

Among high-skilled migrants in the EU, ICT represents one of the largest shares of occupation for migrants coming mostly from non-EU countries but also from EU15 and NMS13. In recent years, ICT has become the largest occupation for qualified male immigrants in the EU (figure 2.9, panel b). The technological boom since the early 2000s has led to a rapid increase in the share of households with internet access, from 20 percent in 2000 to about 90 percent in 2019. This trend in demand for ICT services has brought about significant increases in the number of ICT professionals in all EU countries (figure 2.10, panel a). In this context, many EU countries rely heavily on foreign workers to fill vacancy needs in the sector. Northern EU15 countries, in particular, have seen the share of migrants in ICT occupations increase, from 10 percent in 2004 to close to 20 percent in 2018 (figure 2.10, panel b). In contrast, migrant ICT professionals represent less than 10 percent of foreign-born workers in southern EU15 countries (Greece, Italy, Portugal, and Spain), and about 5 percent in New Member States. The large influx of migrant ICT workers has come mostly from non-EU countries, in particular from South Asia. Migrants from other EU15 countries represent 4 percent of ICT workers in northern EU15 countries, and migrants from NMS13 countries account for an additional 2 percent. Although they represent a smaller share of ICT migrant workers, more than 200,000 ICT professionals from NMS13 countries worked in other EU countries in 2018,

FIGURE 2.9

Top 10 occupations of highly educated workers in the European Union, 2018

a. Male natives

Occupation	Share of total employment (%)
214 Engineering professional	
251 Software and app developer	
311 Physical/engineering science technician	
242 Administration professional	
233 Secondary education teacher	
132 Manuf/distribution manager	
241 Finance professional	
243 Sales/marketing/PR	
332 Sales/purchasing agent	
261 Legal professional	

b. Male NMS13 immigrants

Occupation	Share of total employment (%)
251 Software and app developer	
214 Engineering professional	
711 Building frame worker	
311 Physical/engineering technician	
833 Heavy truck/bus driver	
221 Medical doctor	
712 Building finisher	
933 Transportation worker	
723 Machinery mechanic	
132 Manuf manager	

c. Female natives

Occupation	Share of total employment (%)
234 Primary school/ early childhood teacher	
233 Secondary education teacher	
263 Social/religious professional	
222 Nurse/midwife	
242 Administration professional	
334 Administrative/secretary	
341 Legal/social associate professional	
226 Other health professional	
235 Other teaching professional	
522 Shop salesperson	

d. Female NMS13 immigrants

Occupation	Share of total employment (%)
911 Cleaner/helper	
532 Personal care worker	
522 Shop salesperson	
221 Medical doctor	
242 Administration professional	
441 Clerical support	
513 Waiter/bartender	
334 Administrative/secretary	
322 Nurse associate	
341 Legal/social assoc	

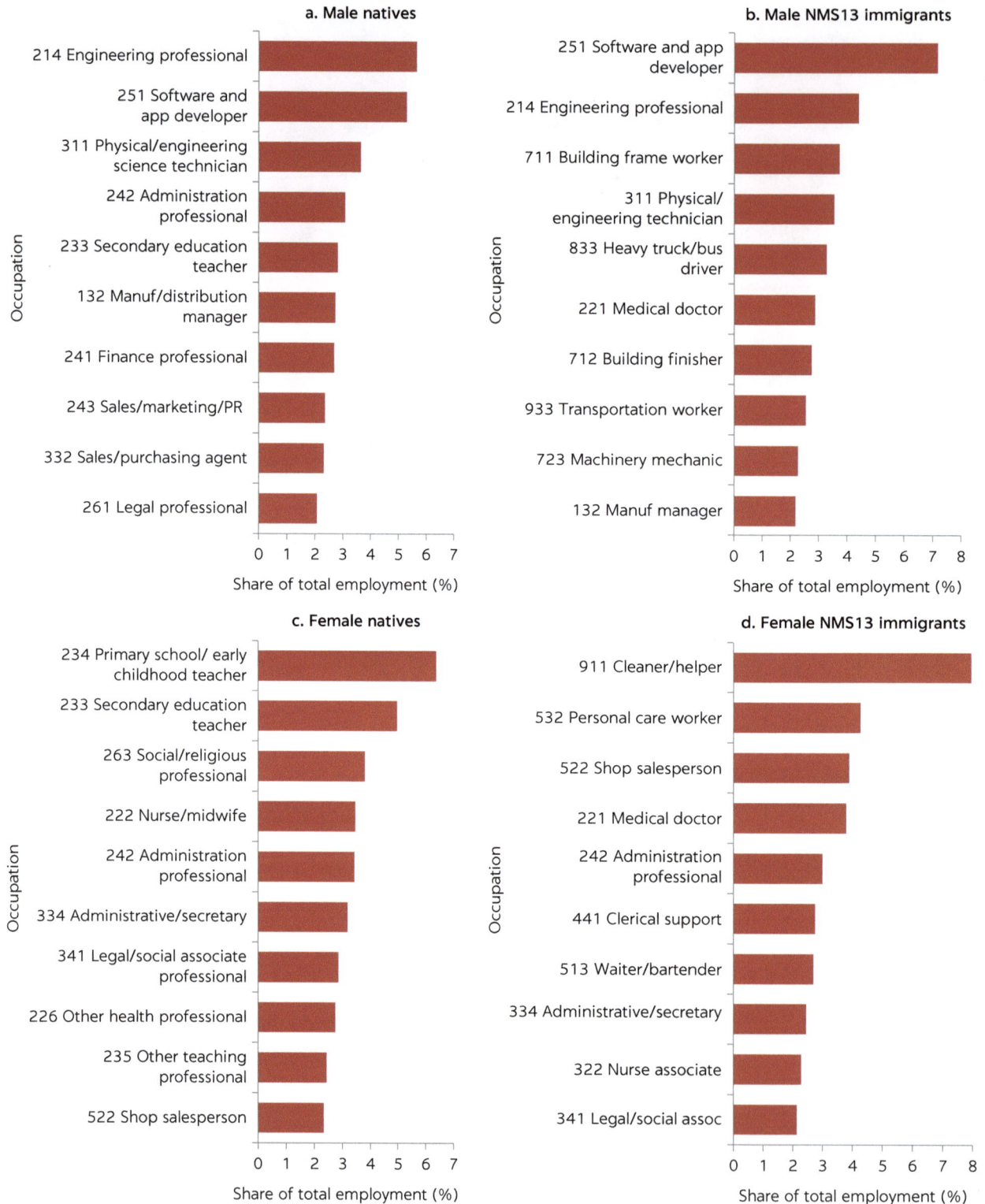

Source: Estimates based on data from the European Union Labour Force Survey (database).
Note: NMS13 = New Member States joining in 2004, 2007, and 2013 (Bulgaria, Croatia, Cyprus, the Czech Republic, Estonia, Hungary, Latvia, Lithuania, Malta, Poland, Romania, the Slovak Republic, and Slovenia).

FIGURE 2.10

ICT workers in European Union countries, 2004–18

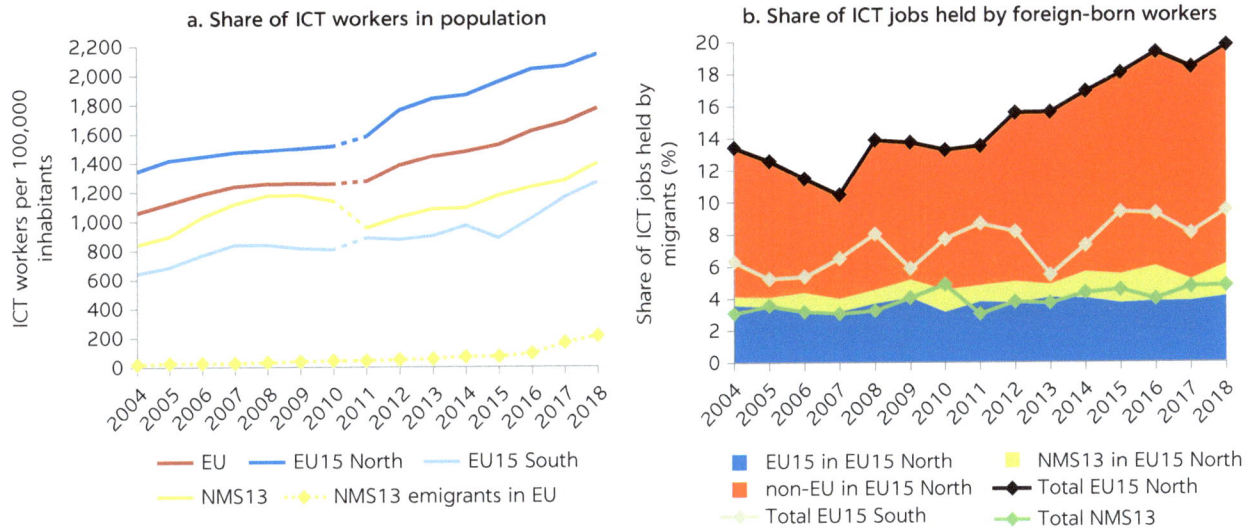

a. Share of ICT workers in population

b. Share of ICT jobs held by foreign-born workers

Source: Estimates based on data from the European Union Labour Force Survey (database) and Eurostat (online data code: isoc_sks_itspt).
Notes: The break in the series in 2011 is due to the change in the categorization of occupations (from ISCO-88 to ISCO-08). EU15 = European Union members before 2004 (Austria, Belgium, Denmark, Finland, France, Germany, Greece, Ireland, Italy, Luxembourg, the Netherlands, Portugal, Spain, Sweden, and the United Kingdom); EU North = northern EU members before 2004 (Austria, Belgium, Denmark, Finland, France, Germany, Ireland, Luxembourg, the Netherlands, Sweden, and the United Kingdom); EU15 South = EU members before 2004 from the Mediterranean (Greece, Italy, Portugal, and Spain); ICT = information and communication technology; ISCO = International Standard Classification of Occupations; NMS13 = New Member States joining in 2004, 2007, and 2013 (Bulgaria, Croatia, Cyprus, the Czech Republic, Estonia, Hungary, Latvia, Lithuania, Malta, Poland, Romania, the Slovak Republic, and Slovenia).

mostly in the West, representing 15 percent of the total stock of ICT workers at origin. However, the overall supply of ICT workers in NMS13 countries has followed upward trends similar to those in EU15 countries, so the gap between the two subregions has not widened as a result of this high-skilled emigration.

NOTES

1. Migrants are defined in this report as individuals who were born in a different country from their current country of residence. From the perspective of receiving countries, immigrants are those born in a third country, while from the perspective of sending countries, emigrants are natives (born in the sending country) that reside in a third country.

2. The EU15's full membership before 2004 and as of January 1, 2020, consisted of Austria, Belgium, Denmark, Finland, France, Germany, Greece, Ireland, Italy, Luxembourg, the Netherlands, Portugal, Spain, Sweden, and the United Kingdom.

3. The NMS13 (with year of accession) consists of the following: Cyprus, the Czech Republic, Estonia, Hungary, Latvia, Lithuania, Malta, Poland, the Slovak Republic, and Slovenia (2004); Bulgaria and Romania (2007); and Croatia (2013).

4. The EFTA consists of Andorra, Channel Islands, Faroe Islands, Gibraltar, Greenland, Holy See, Iceland, Isle of Man, Liechtenstein, Monaco, Norway, San Marino, and Switzerland.

5. The EU28 represents the full EU membership as of January 1, 2020, before the withdrawal of the United Kingdom (Brexit)—that is, the EU15 plus the NMS13.

6. Using the International Labour Organization's International Standard Classification of Occupations structure. For more information, see https://www.ilo.org/public/english/bureau/stat/isco/isco08/.

REFERENCES

Aleksynska, Mariya, and Ahmed Tritah. 2013. "Occupation–Education Mismatch of Immigrant Workers in Europe: Context and Policies." *Economics of Education Review* 36 (October): 229–44.

Borjas, George J. 2015. "The Slowdown in the Economic Assimilation of Immigrants: Aging and Cohort Effects Revisited Again." *Journal of Human Capital* 9 (4): 483–517.

Card, David, and Thomas Lemieux. 2001. "Can Falling Supply Explain the Rising Return to College for Younger Men? A Cohort-Based Analysis." *Quarterly Journal of Economics* 116 (2): 705–46.

Cortes, Kalena E. 2004. "Are Refugees Different from Economic Immigrants? Some Empirical Evidence on the Heterogeneity of Immigrant Groups in the United States." *Review of Economics and Statistics* 86 (2): 465–80.

Docquier, Frédéric, Riccardo Turati, Jérôme Valette, and Chrysovalantis Vasilakis. 2018. "Birthplace Diversity and Economic Growth: Evidence from the US States in the Post–World War II Period." IZA Discussion Paper 11802, Institute of Labor Economics, Bonn.

Draženović, I., M. Kunovac, and D. Pripužić. 2018. "Dynamics and Determinants of Migration: The Case of Croatia and Experience of New EU Member States." Croatian National Bank (HNB), Zagreb.

European Commission. 2021. *Annual Report on Intra-EU Labour Mobility 2020*. Luxembourg: European Union. doi:10.2767/075264.

Friedberg, Rachel M. 2000. "You Can't Take It with You? Immigrant Assimilation and the Portability of Human Capital." *Journal of Labor Economics* 18 (2): 221–51.

Gruber, E., I. Sarajlic Vukovic, M. Musovic, D. Moravek, B. Starcevic, S. Martic Biocina, and R. Knez. 2020. "Migration of Croatian Physicians in the Global Context." *Medicina Fluminensis* (56) 2: 88–96.

Jurić, T. 2017. "Suvremeno iseljavanje Hrvata u Njemačku: Karakteristike i motivi." *Migracijske i etničke teme* 24 (3): 337–71.

Munoz Boudet, Ana Maria, Lourdes Rodriguez Chamussy, Christina Chiarella, and Isil Oral Savonitto. 2021. "Women and STEM in Europe and Central Asia." World Bank, Washington, DC.

National Bank of Poland. 2019. "Information from Surveys of Immigrants in Bydgoszcz and Wrocław in 2018 and 2019" (in Polish). National Bank of Poland, Warsaw. https://www.nbp.pl/publikacje/migracyjne/raport_imigranci_Bydgoszcz_Wroclaw_2019.pdf.

Peri, Giovanni, and Chad Sparber. 2011. "Highly Educated Immigrants and Native Occupational Choice." *Industrial Relations: A Journal of Economy and Society* 50 (3): 385–411.

Ridao-Cano, Cristobal, and Christian Bodewig. 2018. "Growing United: Upgrading Europe's Convergence Machine." World Bank Report on the European Union, World Bank, Washington, DC.

Statistics Poland. 2020a. "The Demand for Labour in 2019." Warszawa, Bydgoszcz. https://stat.gov.pl/en/topics/labour-market/demand-for-labor/the-demand-for-labour-in-2019,1,14.html.

Statistics Poland. 2020b. "The Foreign Population in Poland during the COVID-19 Pandemic." Warszawa, Bydgoszcz. https://stat.gov.pl/en/experimental-statistics/human-capital/the-foreign-population-in-poland-during-the-covid-19-pandemic,10,1.html.

Union of Entrepreneurs and Employers. 2018. "Realizacja Czarnego Scenariusza: Czy Polska Straci Pracownikow z Ukrainy na Rzecz Niemiec?" Warszawa. http://zpp.net.pl/wp-content/uploads/2018/12/Memorandum.pdf.

Župarić-Iljić, D. 2016. "Emigration from the Republic of Croatia after the Accession to the European Union." Friedrich Ebert Stiftung, Zagreb.

Župarić-Iljić, D., and M. Bara. 2014. "Unutrašnje i vanjske migracije u Hrvatskoj: povijesni i suvremeni kontekst." In *Migracije i razvoj Hrvatske: Podloga za hrvatsku migracijsku strategiju*, edited by V. Puljiz, J. Tica, and D. Vidović, 197–213. Croatian Chamber of Economy, Zagreb.

3 Drivers of Migration within the European Union

WAGE AND EMPLOYMENT GAPS

Wage gaps between migrant-sending and migrant-receiving countries in the European Union (EU) are significant and closely associated with migration patterns. Wage gaps create a strong incentive for workers in less economically developed regions to migrate in search of better living standards. Empirical evidence shows that most migrants move in search of better economic opportunities and that income gaps are a key factor of bilateral migration flows (World Bank 2018). In several New Member States (NMS13)—such as Bulgaria, Croatia, Latvia, Lithuania, and Romania—annual earnings are about half the average in the EU28 (figure 3.1, panel a).[1] The wage gap is even larger with respect to the most highly developed EU28 countries, particularly Austria, Germany, Luxembourg, the Netherlands, Sweden, and the United Kingdom.

Even if a portion of the wage gaps originates from skill differences, studies have found extremely large earnings gaps among workers with identical skill sets (Clemens, Montenegro, and Pritchett 2019). The largest segment of the wage gaps is explained by the region in which workers are located, rather than by human capital or technological disparities. This has been labeled the *place premium* (Clemens 2013). Thus, countries with higher wages attract more immigration, whereas those with lower wages tend to face migration outflows (see figure 3.1, panel a).

In the same vein, unemployment differentials are strongly correlated with migration flows across Europe. Within countries, regions that suffered from higher unemployment rates in 2002 relative to the national average faced subsequent migration outflows during 2003–17, but the opposite was true in top-performing regions (see figure 3.1, panel b). There is obviously a circular and self-reinforcing relationship between migration outflows and unemployment levels. Regions with high employment levels tend to attract more migrants, who mostly come from regions with high unemployment. Such flows, however, tend to narrow employment gaps. Nevertheless, employment opportunities and place premiums in earnings seem to be at the root of migration flows.

FIGURE 3.1

Earnings, unemployment, and net emigration, European Union, circa 2003–18

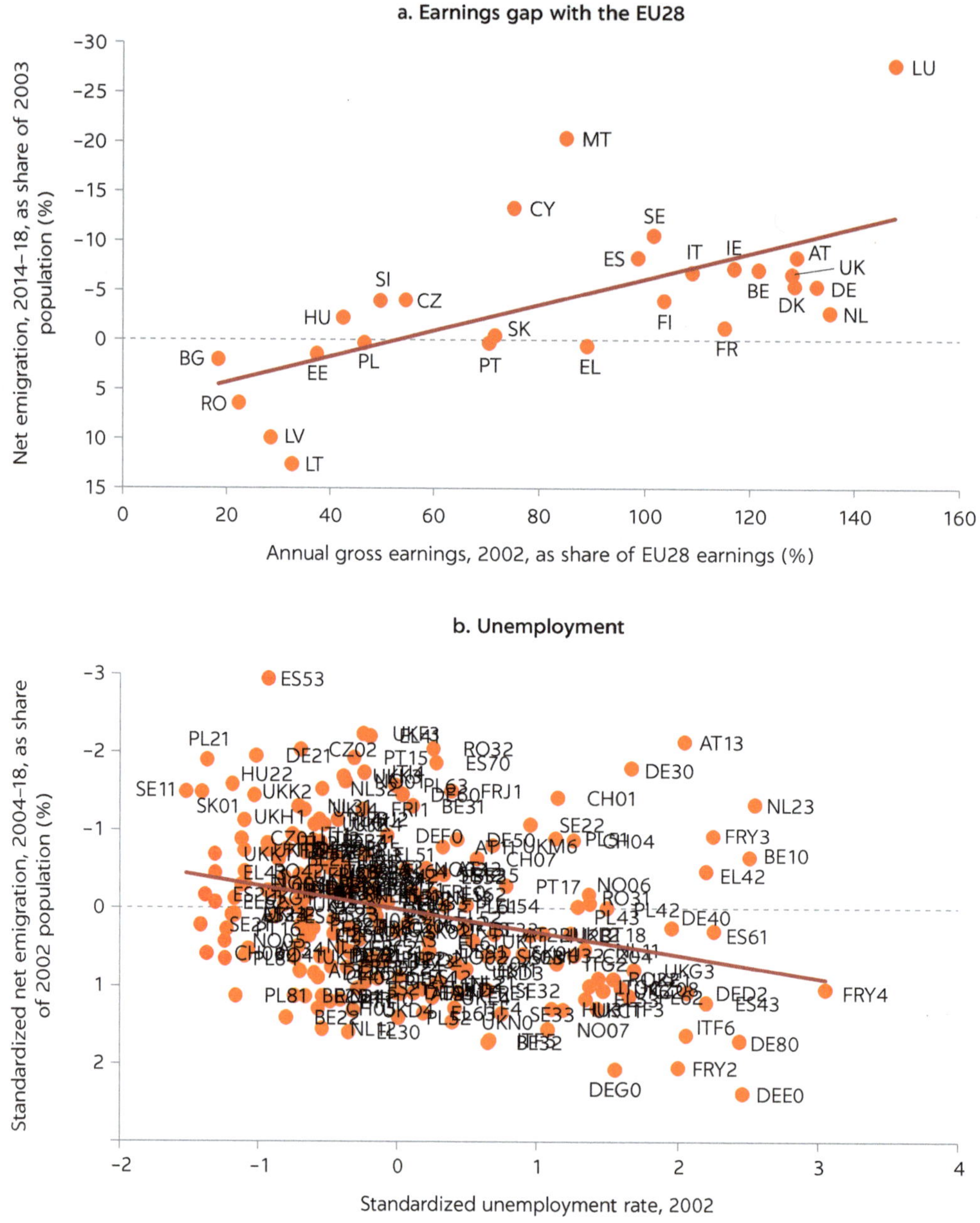

a. Earnings gap with the EU28

b. Unemployment

Sources: Data of Structure of Earnings Survey (database) and Population (database), Eurostat, European Commission.

Note: Standardized unemployment rates and net emigration measures are calculated by dividing the gap between each region and the national average, divided by the standard deviation in each country. Net emigration is defined as the number of emigrants (departures) minus the number of immigrants (arrivals) in a given region and period of time. EU28 = full EU membership before the departure of the United Kingdom in 2020 (Brexit). The labels in panel b show the Nomenclature of Territorial Units for Statistics 2 (NUTS 2) regional code, which includes the Alpha-2 country code and the two-digit principal subdivision code.

TECHNOLOGICAL CHANGE, AUTOMATION, AND "GOOD JOBS"

Technological change and automation are changing the demand for labor and the geography of jobs. This effect is occurring not only in Europe but also across the globe. Over the last decade, there has been a pronounced shift of

FIGURE 3.2

Share of nonroutine cognitive jobs in the European Union, 2012, and net immigration, 2013–17

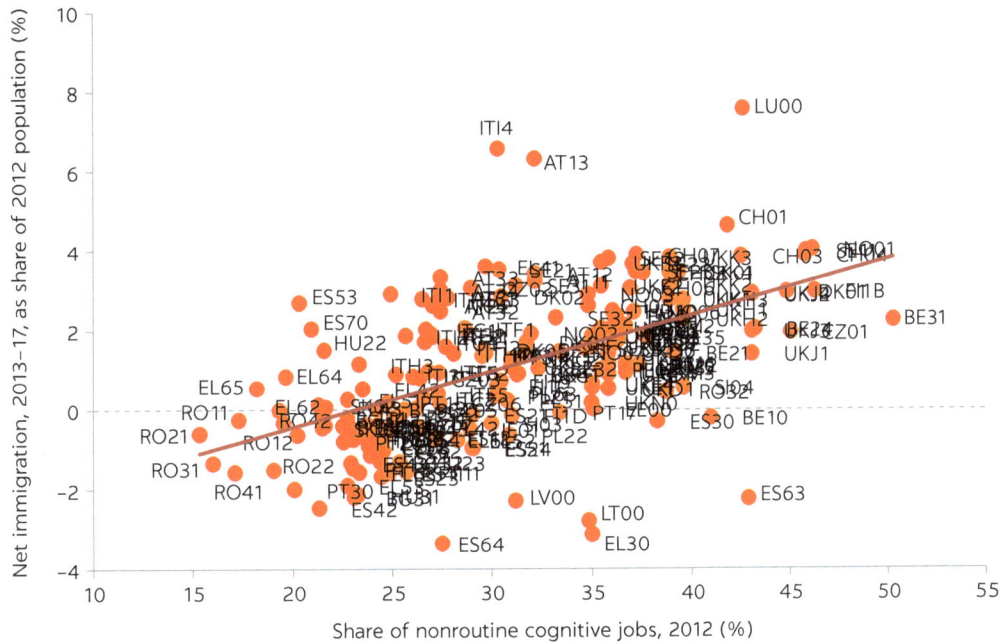

Sources: World Bank elaboration based on data from the European Union Labour Force Survey (database), Eurostat.
Note: Net immigration is defined as the number of immigrants (arrivals) minus the number of emigrants (departures) in a given region and period of time. The labels show the Nomenclature of Territorial Units for Statistics 2 (NUTS 2) regional code, which includes the Alpha-2 country code and the two-digit principal subdivision code.

workers out of routine occupations toward nonroutine occupations across all across all the EU. The process of deroutinization has increased the demand of high-skilled and high-income jobs while reducing that of lower-skilled jobs, increasing the income divide between these two groups (Hoftijzer and Gortazar 2018). Greater opportunities for employment in nonroutine cognitive occupations that require greater skills seem to play a role in attracting migrants. In the EU15 and in the NMS13, there was a positive correlation between the initial share of total employment in nonroutine cognitive occupations in 2012 and the increase in net immigration rates during the subsequent five years (figure 3.2).[2] This may be the result of the regional concentration of higher-skilled, high-paying nonroutine cognitive jobs in urban areas with more human capital, which may have led to more internal and cross-border worker mobility.

DEMOGRAPHIC PATTERNS, NETWORKS, QUALITY OF PUBLIC SERVICES, AND GOVERNANCE

A key driver of migration found in the literature is the existence of networks of previous migrants of the same nationality in the destination country (Clark, Hatton, and Williamson 2007). These diasporas explain the majority of variability in migration flows (Beine, Docquier, and Özden 2011), especially in relation to the migration of low-skilled workers. Sharing a common language and culture greatly reduces the economic and psychological costs associated with migration. In particular, migrant networks provide an essential service to newer waves of migrants during their job search process, improving their labor market outcomes in the destination country (Edin, Fredriksson, and Åslund 2003; Munshi 2003).

The quality levels of public services in both origin and the destination countries also constitute push and pull factors for migration. From the perspective of the destination countries, well-performing education and health systems tend to attract migrants (Geis, Uebelmesser, and Werding 2013). Social safety nets can also play a role in attracting migrants from the least developed countries (Pedersen, Pytlikova, and Smith 2008). From the perspective of sending regions, local amenities, in particular security and public services, also play a significant role in shaping intentions to emigrate (Dustmann and Okatenko 2014).

Finally, recent studies find that corruption plays an important role in both increasing emigration and deterring immigration, especially for high-skilled workers. A high level of corruption in a country could significantly discourage immigration, because it is associated with weaker and more volatile economic conditions and more job insecurity (Poprawe 2015). Besides reducing immigration levels, more corruption also has an effect on increasing emigration rates in sending countries (Auer, Römer, and Tjaden 2020). The impact of corruption on emigration rates is larger for high-skilled workers, because it erodes the concept of meritocracy and reduces returns to education (Cooray and Schneider 2016; Dimant, Krieger, and Meierrieks 2013). Therefore, corruption might also affect the selection into migration, exacerbating the "brain drain" from origin countries, and it could also reduce the incentives for migrants to return to their home country after working abroad.

THE MULTIFACETED AND COMPLEX NATURE OF THE DRIVERS OF MIGRATION BEYOND INCOME GAPS

Regression analysis shows that income and labor market gaps are strong drivers of bilateral migration flows. For example, as the gross domestic product (GDP) per capita level rises in a country of destination j relative to a country of origin i, more people move from the latter to the former country (first column of table 3.1).[3] On top of GDP differences, the gap in after-tax annual earnings between countries j and i is also estimated to have a positive effect on migration flows (second column of table 3.1); a 1 percent increase in the ratio of wages between countries j and i is associated with a 0.22 percent increase in migration flows from country i to country j. And, given that a higher inflation rate reduces the real value of wages, the difference in the inflation rate between the destination and sending countries is associated with a reduction in migration flows from the latter to the former country. Last, although the correlation between the gap in unemployment rates and migration flows is measured with less precision, the third column of table 3.1 shows that the larger the relative size of the unemployment rate, the lower the expected migration flows.

Additionally, legal barriers to mobility; the generosity of the welfare system; employment protection legislation; and, as noted earlier, the levels of corruption also matter substantially in the migration decision. The EU accession of the NMS13 in 2004, 2007, and 2013 boosted bilateral migration flows from the east to the west of the EU (World Bank 2019). However, the EU15 countries lifted work restrictions for NMS13 workers at different times—for example Polish citizens received full rights to work in the United Kingdom in 2004, but did not do

TABLE 3.1 **Drivers of bilateral migration flows**

VARIABLE	(1) LOG MIGRATION$_{ij}$	(2) LOG MIGRATION$_{ij}$	(3) LOG MIGRATION$_{ij}$
Contiguous border$_{ijt}$	0.193**	0.221**	−0.134
	(0.079)	(0.092)	(0.098)
Common language$_{ijt}$	1.366***	1.280***	1.096***
	(0.086)	(0.116)	(0.103)
Distance (log)$_{ijt}$	−0.876***	−0.793***	−1.189***
	(0.044)	(0.053)	(0.068)
Common religion$_{ijt}$	1.084***	1.010***	1.035***
	(0.068)	(0.078)	(0.093)
Time zone difference$_{ijt}$	−0.259***	−0.352***	−0.340***
	(0.040)	(0.046)	(0.058)
Population size in i (log)	0.598***	0.625***	0.664***
	(0.012)	(0.015)	(0.033)
Population size in j (log)	0.621***	0.557***	0.677***
	(0.017)	(0.023)	(0.029)
GDP per capita, PPP (j/i), log	1.368***	1.149***	1.095***
	(0.089)	(0.138)	(0.080)
Net earnings (j/i), log		0.206***	
		(0.076)	
Inflation (j/i), log		−0.107***	−0.124***
		(0.018)	(0.019)
Unemployment rate (j/i), log	0.043	0.010	−0.143***
	(0.044)	(0.056)	(0.053)
Share of agriculture (j/i), log	0.012	0.039	
	(0.036)	(0.041)	
Share of services (j/i), log	0.435**	−0.386	
	(0.180)	(0.261)	
Right to work$_{ijt}$	0.802***	−0.113	
	(0.090)	(0.152)	
Urban (j/i), log		0.339***	
		(0.117)	
Social protection spending (j/i)			0.361***
			(0.092)
Product market regulation (j/i), log			0.048
			(0.066)
Employment protection legislation (j/i), log			−0.163**
			(0.068)
Trade (j/i), log			0.178**
			(0.078)
WGI Control of Corruption (j/i), log	0.522***	0.258*	0.531***
	(0.097)	(0.134)	(0.119)
Constant	−3.801***	−3.074***	−2.047***
	(0.350)	(0.408)	(0.439)
Observations	6,053	4,440	3,339
R^2	0.565	0.564	0.585
Year FE	YES	YES	YES

Source: World Bank calculations based on data from the CEPII Gravity Database, migration and labor statistics from the Organisation for Economic Co-operation and Development (OECD), and the World Bank World Development Indicators.

Note: The regression estimates the (log) of migration flows from sending country i to receiving country j in year t. All regressions control for time effects. Explanatory factors besides gravity-type variables are all introduced as the ratio between the receiving country j and the sending country i (j/i). log = logarithm; PPP = purchasing power parity; Right to work$_{ijt}$ = legal right for the population from country i to work in country j; Social protection spending (SPS) (j/i) = (SPS / GDP) in j divided by (SPS / GDP) in i; WGI = Worldwide Governance Indicators. Robust standard errors in parentheses. Significance level: * = 10 percent, ** = 5 percent, *** = 1 percent.

so until 2011 in Germany. When using the full sample that covers the universe of all the sending countries, lifting all work restrictions between two countries in the EU is associated with a 120 percent increase in bilateral migration flows.[4] Another key driver of migration is the relative size of the welfare state. In particular, the larger the social protection expenditures per capita in destination country j relative to sending country i, the more people tend to migrate from i to j. The level of protection and rigidity in the labor market also affects migration decisions. In particular, larger migration flows are observed from countries with stricter employment protection legislations to countries with more flexible labor arrangements. Furthermore, more pronounced openness in a country—measured by the relative share of trade over total GDP—is associated with a larger migration inflow. Last, measures of the level of corruption in a country, such as the Control of Corruption of the World Bank Worldwide Governance Indicators, are strongly linked with migration flows.[5] Across all specifications, the log of the ratio of the corruption indicators consistently points to the fact that, as the gap in the corruption level between sending and receiving countries increases, more people migrate. More specifically, a 1 percent widening in the level of corruption between countries i and j (meaning that country i is more corrupt or country j is less corrupt) is associated with a rise in migration flows from country i to country j of about 0.5 percent.

NOTES

1. The NMS13 (with year of accession) consists of the following: Cyprus, the Czech Republic, Estonia, Hungary, Latvia, Lithuania, Malta, Poland, the Slovak Republic, and Slovenia (2004); Bulgaria and Romania (2007); and Croatia (2013). The EU28 represents the full EU membership before the departure of the United Kingdom in 2020 (Brexit)—that is, the original 15 members (Austria, Belgium, Denmark, Finland, France, Germany, Greece, Ireland, Italy, Luxembourg, the Netherlands, Portugal, Spain, Sweden, and the United Kingdom) plus the NMS13.
2. The EU15's full membership before 2004 consisted of Austria, Belgium, Denmark, Finland, France, Germany, Greece, Ireland, Italy, Luxembourg, the Netherlands, Portugal, Spain, Sweden, and the United Kingdom.
3. The methodology to estimate the gravity equation whose results are reported in table 3.1 is detailed in appendix B.
4. As the dependent variable is log-transformed, to obtain the exact impact on the right-to-work variable, the coefficient presented in column 1 (that is, 0.80) must also be transformed according to the formula exp(0.80) − 1. Furthermore, the coefficient on this variable becomes insignificant in column 2, because data are not available for several New Member States (Bulgaria, Croatia, Latvia, Lithuania, and Romania).
5. Other measures of corruption—such as the Government Effectiveness of the Worldwide Governance Indicators, the Corruption Perception Index of Transparency International, and the Corruption score of the International Country Risk Guide—yield similarly strong correlations between corruption levels and migration flows.

REFERENCES

Auer, Daniel, Friederike Römer, and Jasper Tjaden. 2020. "Corruption and the Desire to Leave: Quasi-Experimental Evidence on Corruption as a Driver of Emigration Intentions." *IZA Journal of Development and Migration* 11 (1): 7.

Beine, Michel, Frederic Docquier, and Çağlar Özden. 2011. "Diasporas." *Journal of Development Economics* 95: 30–41.

Clark, X., T. J. Hatton, and J. G. Williamson. 2007. "Explaining US Immigration, 1971–1998." *Review of Economics and Statistics* 89 (2): 359–73.

Clemens, Michael A. 2013. "Why Do Programmers Earn More in Houston Than Hyderabad? Evidence from Randomized Processing of US Visas." *American Economic Review* 103 (3): 198–202.

Clemens, Michael A., Claudio E. Montenegro, and Lant Pritchett. 2019. "The Place Premium: Bounding the Price Equivalent of Migration Barriers." *Review of Economics and Statistics* 101 (2): 201–13.

Cooray, Arusha, and Friedrich Schneider. 2016. "Does Corruption Promote Emigration? An Empirical Examination." *Journal of Population Economics* 29: 293–310.

Dimant, Eugen, Tim Krieger, and Daniel Meierrieks. 2013. "The Effect of Corruption on Migration, 1985–2000." *Applied Economics Letters* 20 (13): 1270–74.

Dustmann, Christian, and Anna Okatenko. 2014. "Out-migration, Wealth Constraints, and the Quality of Local Amenities." *Journal of Development Economics* 110 (September): 52–63.

Edin, Per-Anders, Peter Fredriksson, and Olof Åslund. 2003. "Ethnic Enclaves and the Economic Success of Immigrants—Evidence from a Natural Experiment." *Quarterly Journal of Economics* 118 (1): 329–57.

Geis, Wido, Silke Uebelmesser, and Martin Werding. 2013. "How Do Migrants Choose Their Destination Country? An Analysis of Institutional Determinants." *Review of International Economics* 21 (5): 825–40.

Hoftijzer, Margo, and Lucas Gortazar. 2018. "Skills and Europe's Labor Market: How Technological Change and Other Drivers of Skill Demand and Supply are Shaping Europe's Labor Market." World Bank, Washington, DC.

Munshi, Kaivan. 2003. "Networks in the Modern Economy: Mexican Migrants in the U.S. Labor Market." *Quarterly Journal of Economics* 118 (2): 549–97.

Pedersen, P. J., M. Pytlikova, and N. Smith. 2008. "Selection and Network Effects—Migration Flows into OECD Countries 1990–2000." *European Economic Review* 52 (7): 1160–86.

Poprawe, Marie. 2015. "On the Relationship between Corruption and Migration: Empirical Evidence from a Gravity Model of Migration." *Public Choice* 163 (3–4): 337–54.

World Bank. 2018. *Moving for Prosperity: Global Migration and Labor Markets*. Policy Research Report. Washington, DC: World Bank.

World Bank. 2019. "Migration and Brain Drain" (in Turkish). Europe and Central Asia Economic Update, Office of the Chief Economist, World Bank, Washington, DC.

4 The Impact of Migration on Receiving Countries and Regions

IMMIGRATION'S POSITIVE IMPACT ON GROWTH

Most empirical studies of the relationship between immigration and economic growth in European migrant-receiving countries find a positive relationship. However, results vary depending on the methodology, time frame, and country sample (Rutledge and Kane 2018). In theoretical analyses, the impact of immigration varies depending on the skill level of the migrant population, with high-skilled immigration having larger benefits for growth (Borjas 2019; Dolado, Goria, and Ichino 1994). Cross-country empirical studies on Europe come to a similar conclusion. Studies using cross-country analysis by the Organisation for Economic Co-operation and Development (OECD) typically find that immigration has a positive impact on growth in receiving countries (Aleksynska and Tritah 2015; Alesina, Harnoss, and Rapoport 2016; Boubtane, Dumont, and Rault 2016; Felbermayr, Hiller, and Sala 2010; Jaumotte, Koloskova, and Saxena 2016). A smaller number of earlier studies by the OECD—such as Dolado, Goria, and Ichino (1994) for the period 1960–85 and Orefice (2010) for the period 1998–2007—find evidence of a negative impact of immigration on gross domestic product (GDP) per capita.[1] Both studies also show, however, that high-skilled immigration has a positive effect on GDP per capita, which partly compensates for the overall negative effects of immigration on GDP per capita. Thus, the effect of immigration on GDP per capita depends on the skill composition of migrants. It has also been shown to depend on the characteristics of the country of destination (Kang and Kim 2012; Orefice 2010).

Empirical studies focusing on individual countries in the European Union (EU) also find that immigration exerts positive effects on growth. Muysken and Ziesemer (2011) look at the macroeconomic impact of both aging and immigration on economic growth. Using data from the Netherlands from 1973 to 2009, they find that immigration helps alleviate the aging problem in the long run as long as immigrants are able to participate in the labor force at least as much as the native population does. As in cross-country studies, they also highlight that the more educated the immigrants are or become, the greater their contribution to growth. In a study of France, d'Albis, Boubtane, and

Coulibaly (2015) use a database in which immigration is measured by the flow of freshly issued long-term residence permits. Using a model estimation of monthly data over 1994–2008, they find that immigration has increased France's GDP per capita over the period, particularly in the case of family immigration. Other studies of individual countries outside Europe, such as Docquier et al. (2018) on the United States, also find that immigration has positive effects on economic growth.

Immigration, especially high-skilled immigration, can affect growth through three main channels: labor input, capital accumulation, and productivity. A consistent inflow of high-skilled migrants can push a country toward the adoption of new technologies (Chander and Thangavelu 2004). Some studies also highlighted that a marginal increase in the stock of skilled human capital as a result of immigration contributes more to productivity growth the closer a country is to the technological frontier (Lodigiani 2008; Vandenbussche, Aghion, and Meghir 2006). Cross-country macro studies find no effect or a negative effect of immigration on productivity in receiving countries (Docquier and Rapoport 2009; Ortega and Peri 2009, 2014). In contrast, studies using firm-level data for individual countries in Europe typically find positive effects on firm productivity in France (Mitaritonna, Orefice, and Peri 2017) and the United Kingdom (Ottaviano, Peri, and Wright 2018) but no effect in Germany (Trax, Brunow, and Suedekum 2015). A causal, positive impact of immigration on innovation, measured by the number of registered patents, has also been evidenced (Burchardi et al. 2020; Hunt and Gauthier-Loiselle 2010). Regarding capital accumulation, the share of highly educated immigrants has been shown to add to capital accumulation (Ortega and Peri 2009).

IMPLICATIONS FOR POPULATION GROWTH, DEMOGRAPHIC COMPOSITION, AND AGING

Immigration has made a strong contribution to population growth in EU15 countries since the mid-1990s.[2] From 1995 to 2017, the population in the EU15 grew by an average of 9.6 percent. This is lower than the rates in most other developed countries, such as Australia (36.0 percent), New Zealand (30.0 percent), Canada (25.0 percent), the United States (22.0 percent), and the Republic of Korea (14.0 percent). Net immigration inflows accounted for close to 80 percent of the growth (figure 4.1, panel a), providing a vital boost to an otherwise stagnant natural growth rate.

Immigration also has important implications for a country's age structure. Immigrants in the EU15 tend to be younger than natives. Migrants are disproportionately of working age, given that their main driver for migration is economic opportunity. In high-income EU destination countries with aging populations, migrants help increase the size and share of the working-age population (World Bank 2019). However, at current rates, immigration can contribute only slightly to any reduction in aging among receiving countries. The old-age dependency ratio—the ratio between the population age 65 and older and the working-age population, age 15–64—stood at 30 percent in EU15 countries in 2015. If recent migration trends continue, it is projected to

FIGURE 4.1

Change in population, European Union, 1995–2017

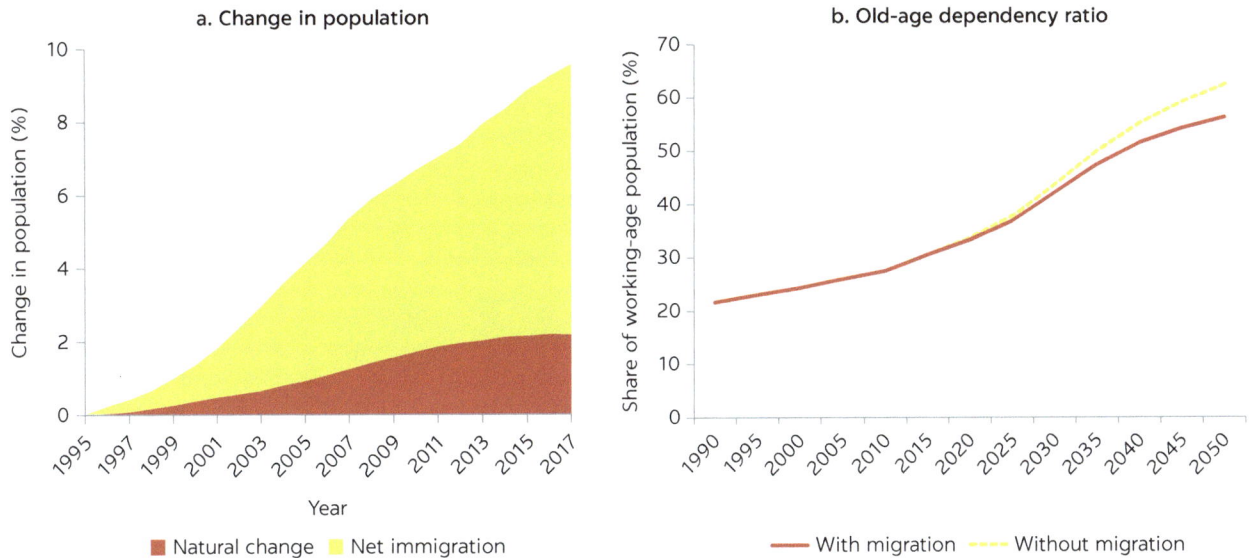

Sources: Elaboration based on Lutz et al. 2018; data from Population (database), Eurostat, European Commission, https://ec.europa.eu/eurostat/web/population/overview; Wittgenstein Center Human Capital Data Explorer, Wittgenstein Center for Demography and Global Human Capital, http://www.wittgensteincentre.org/dataexplorer.
Note: Net immigration is defined as the difference between immigration flows (arrivals) and emigration flows (departures) in a given European region. Natural change is the difference between the number of live births and deaths during a given time period.

reach 56 percent by 2050, which is only slightly lower than the rate estimated in a scenario without immigration (figure 4.1, panel b).

IMMIGRATION'S EFFECT ON THE STOCK, VARIETY, AND QUALITY OF HUMAN CAPITAL

Migrant-receiving countries and regions tend to exhibit larger gains in human capital. Despite advances in educational attainment in all but four Nomenclature of Territorial Units for Statistics 2 (NUTS 2) regions during the last decade and a half, gains have been larger in regions with greater net immigration flows (that is, more inflows than outflows) and smaller in migrant-sending regions (figure 4.2). This pattern has been observed in both Western Europe and in the 13 New Member States (NMS13) joining the EU since 2004, and it may derive from various factors, such as the demand for a higher concentration of skills in migrant flows, which incentivized natives to accumulate more skills in migrant-receiving areas, or migrants to accumulate skills in host countries.[3]

The greater and more diverse human capital contributed by immigration raises productivity among local workers. Various studies find that immigrants contribute skills and concentrate in occupations in which they have a comparative advantage (Peri 2012; Peri and Sparber 2009). The diversification of skills and the focus of migrants on tasks that they are better able to perform boost productivity in the economy and spur innovation. This boost favors natives who specialize in occupations involving communication-intensive tasks.

FIGURE 4.2

Net emigration and changes in tertiary educational attainment, European Union, 2004–17

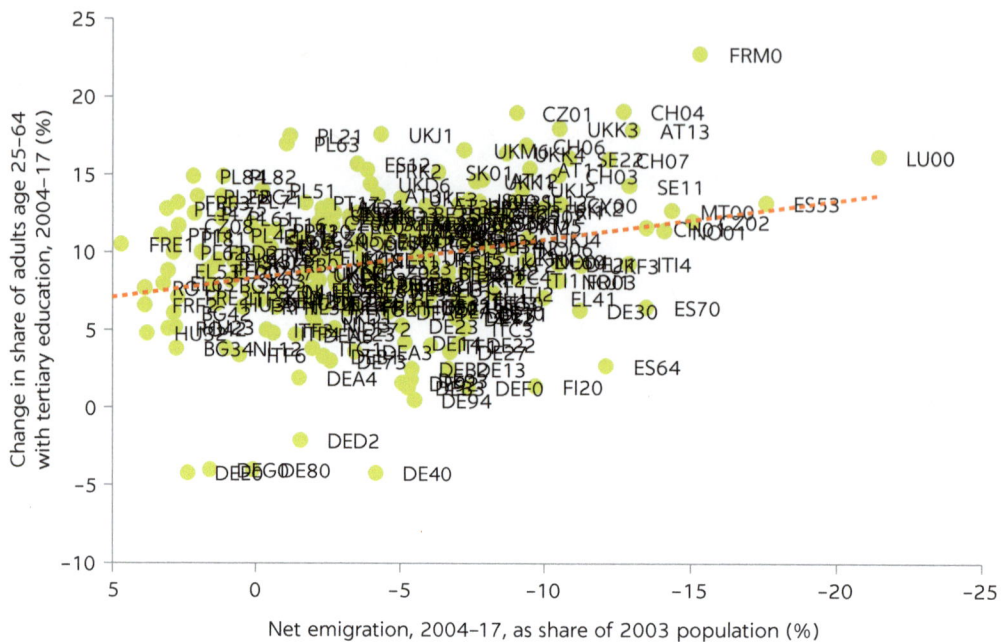

Source: Elaboration based on data from Education and Training (database), Eurostat, European Commission, https://ec.europa.eu/eurostat/web/education-and-training/overview; Population (database), Eurostat, European Commission, https://ec.europa.eu/eurostat/web/population/overview.
Note: Net emigration is defined as the number of emigrants (departures) minus the number of immigrants (arrivals) in a given region and period of time. The labels show the Nomenclature of Territorial Units for Statistics 2 (NUTS 2) regional code, which includes the Alpha-2 country code and the two-digit principal subdivision code.

IMPACTS ON LABOR MARKETS AND PUBLIC FINANCES

Changes in the age and skill composition of the native workforce have been found to be the main drivers of the wage dynamics observed in OECD countries from 2000 to 2010, whereas labor migration has played a much more modest role (Docquier et al. 2018). Overall, older high-skilled workers have been affected the most negatively by changes in the age-education structure of the native population. Because of the rapid aging and educational upgrading in the labor market, these workers face growing competition. Meanwhile, skilled-biased technological change has been a far stronger force in shaping labor market outcomes. As a result, wages of low-skilled younger workers have shown net declines. The issue is that their wages would have declined even more if not for the demographic trends benefiting younger and less-educated workers.

In migrant-receiving countries, immigration has had a small but generally positive effect on domestic wage dynamics and labor supply (Docquier et al. 2018). Immigration in the OECD tends to boost the wages of low-skilled workers, who complement high-skilled workers because net immigration flows tend to be more highly skilled (Docquier, Özden, and Peri 2014). Thus, immigration has reinforced the positive effects of aging and upskilling on low-skilled workers in receiving countries. In more open economies that exercise skill-based migration policies, the positive effects of immigration on low-skilled workers have been more pronounced. However, whereas the benefits of immigration are more likely to be diffused across the population and become more apparent in the longer term, the costs related to displacement or wage decline are more immediate and are concentrated in specific groups of workers (World Bank 2019).

The EU's enlargement led to sizable emigration from some of the new members in Eastern Europe to those in Western Europe; however, the impact on employment and wages of the native population in receiving countries has been subdued. For example, 9 percent of all workers in Lithuania, 6 percent in Latvia and the Slovak Republic, and 5 percent in Poland received work permits in Ireland and the United Kingdom after the EU's enlargement (Elsner 2011). Most of these emigrants were young and had medium to high educational attainment (Zaiceva and Zimmermann 2008). Most studies of receiving countries do not find large effects of the immigration wave on wages and employment (Barrett 2009; Blanchflower and Shadforth 2009). In receiving countries, studies of Lithuania and Poland, where emigration has been widespread, find positive short-term effects of that emigration on wages at home (Dustmann, Frattini, and Rosso 2015; Elsner 2013). These patterns are consistent with the equilibrating effects of migration flows from low- to high-wage (and employment) regions.

Immigration helps address demand shortages in the labor markets of receiving countries, but it has limited effects on the earnings of natives (World Bank 2018). Shortages of workers in specific occupations requiring relevant qualifications and tasks are a challenge to competitiveness in several European economies. Among EU countries, 21 have produced lists of occupations in which shortages are binding; in 10 of these countries, the lists are used as an explicit instrument for determining admissions of workers from other countries (European Commission 2015). Demand shortages vary from country to country. They are more frequently observed in low-skilled occupations—such as machine operators, cleaners, and farm laborers—and in services meeting the growing needs of an aging population (nurses, social service workers, and personal care workers). Although the arrival of migrants may have short-run negative effects on the wages of natives with similar skills, the overall effects are close to zero, and the effects on the wages of natives with complementary skills are typically positive.[4] In the longer term, immigration can boost productivity, promote occupational upgrades, and boost the wages of natives (Ottaviano and Peri 2012).

The fiscal impact of immigrants is broadly neutral or slightly positive in most OECD countries, indicating that immigrants tend to be net contributors to tax and social insurance systems in destination countries (OECD 2013). The net fiscal contribution of immigration normally lies within the range of plus or minus 1 percent of GDP (Rowthorn 2008). For Europe specifically, migrant workers have been estimated to make a net contribution of approximately €42 billion to the national tax and benefit systems of a selected group of 13 EU countries as of 2006 (Barbone, Bontch-Osmolovsky, and Zaidi 2009). Similar positive net effects have been found for France (Chojnicki 2013), the United Kingdom (Dustmann and Frattini 2014; Vargas-Silva 2016), and the Scandinavian countries (Hansen, Schultz-Nielsen, and Tranæs 2017).[5] These fiscal effects of immigration tend to be more positive in the case of high-skilled migrants and migrants from the European Economic Area than in the case of less-skilled migrants and migrants from developing countries (Dustmann and Frattini 2014; Hansen, Schultz-Nielsen, and Tranæs 2017).

NOTES

1. The divergence in findings from more recent studies may be partly explained by differences in time period and sample composition, as well as the difficulties in identifying a causal relationship between immigration and growth. Among available studies, Alesina, Harnoss, and Rapoport 2016; Dolado, Goria, and Ichino 1994; Felbermayr, Hiller, and Sala 2010; and Orefice 2010 use methodologies that are the closest to identifying a causal relationship.
2. The EU15's, the full membership before 2004 consisted of Austria, Belgium, Denmark, Finland, France, Germany, Greece, Ireland, Italy, Luxembourg, the Netherlands, Portugal, Spain, Sweden, and the United Kingdom.
3. The NMS13 (with year of accession) consists of the following: Cyprus, the Czech Republic, Estonia, Hungary, Latvia, Lithuania, Malta, Poland, the Slovak Republic, and Slovenia (2004); Bulgaria and Romania (2007); and Croatia (2013).
4. See Longhi, Nijkamp, and Poot (2005) and Peri (2014) for a meta-analysis of the literature on the impact of immigration on the wages of natives.
5. These accounting exercises that assign a dollar value to the fiscal contribution of migrants rely on a number of assumptions that may be debated (Borjas 1994).

REFERENCES

Aleksynska, Mariya, and Ahmed Tritah. 2015. "The Heterogeneity of Immigrants, Host Countries' Income, and Productivity: A Channel Accounting Approach." *Economic Inquiry* 53 (1): 150–72.

Alesina, Alberto Francesco, Johann Daniel Harnoss, and Hillel Rapoport. 2016. "Birthplace Diversity and Economic Prosperity." *Journal of Economic Growth* 21 (2): 101–38.

Barbone, Luca, Misha Bontch-Osmolovsky, and Salman Zaidi. 2009. "The Foreign-Born Population in the European Union and Its Contribution to National Tax and Benefit Systems: Some Insights from Recent Household Survey Data." Policy Research Working Paper 4899, World Bank, Washington, DC.

Barrett, Alan. 2009. "EU Enlargement and Ireland's Labour Market." IZA Discussion Paper DP 4260, Institute of Labor Economics, Bonn.

Blanchflower, David G., and Chris Shadforth. 2009. "Fear, Unemployment, and Migration." *Economic Journal* 119 (535): F136–F182.

Borjas, George J. 1994. "The Economic Benefits from Immigration." NBER Working Paper 4955, National Bureau of Economic Research, Cambridge, MA.

Borjas, George J. 2019. "Immigration and Economic Growth." NBER Working Paper 25836, National Bureau of Economic Research, Cambridge, MA.

Boubtane, Ekrame, Jean-Christophe Dumont, and Christophe Rault. 2016. "Immigration and Economic Growth in the OECD Countries, 1986–2006." *Oxford Economic Papers* 68 (2): 340–60.

Burchardi, Konrad B., Thomas Chaney, Tarek Alexander Hassan, Lisa Tarquinio, and Stephen Terry. 2020. "Immigration, Innovation, and Growth." CEPR Discussion Paper DP14719, Centre for Economic Policy Research, London.

Chander, Parkash, and Shandre M. Thangavelu. 2004. "Technology Adoption, Education, and Immigration Policy." *Journal of Development Economics* 75 (1): 79–94.

Chojnicki, Xavier. 2013. "The Fiscal Impact of Immigration in France: A Generational Accounting Approach." *World Economy* 36 (8): 1065–90.

d'Albis, Hippolyte, Ekrame Boubtane, and Dramane Coulibaly. 2015. "Immigration Policy and Macroeconomic Performance in France." Etudes et Documents CERDI 5 (March), Center for the Study and Research on International Development, Clermont-Ferrand University, Clermont-Ferrand, France.

Docquier, Frédéric, Çağlar Özden, and Giovanni Peri. 2014. "The Labour Market Effects of Immigration and Emigration in OECD Countries." *VoxEU*, October 6. https://voxeu.org /article/labour-market-effects-migration-oecd-countries.

Docquier, Frédéric, and Hillel Rapoport. 2009. "Documenting the Brain Drain of 'La Crème de la Crème': Three Case-Studies on International Migration at the Upper Tail of the Education Distribution." *Journal of Economics and Statistics* 229 (6): 679–705.

Docquier, Frédéric, Riccardo Turati, Jérôme Valette, and Chrysovalantis Vasilakis. 2018. "Birthplace Diversity and Economic Growth: Evidence from the US States in the Post–World War II Period." IZA Discussion Paper 11802, Institute of Labor Economics, Bonn.

Dolado, Juan J., Alessandra Goria, and Andrea Ichino. 1994. "Immigration, Human Capital, and Growth in the Host Country: Evidence from Pooled Country Data." *Journal of Population Economics* 7 (2): 193–215.

Dustmann, Christian, and Tommaso Frattini. 2014. "The Fiscal Effects of Immigration to the UK." *Economic Journal* 124 (580): F593–F643.

Dustmann, Christian, Tommaso Frattini, and Anna Cecilia Rosso. 2015. "The Effect of Emigration from Poland on Polish Wages." *Scandinavian Journal of Economics* 117 (2): 522–64.

Elsner, Benjamin. 2011. "Emigration and Wages: The EU Enlargement Experiment." IZA Discussion Paper 6111, Institute of Labor Economics, Bonn.

Elsner, Benjamin. 2013. "Emigration and Wages: The EU Enlargement Experiment." *Journal of International Economics* 91 (1): 154–63.

European Commission. 2015. "Determining Labour Shortages and the Need for Labour Migration from Third Countries in the EU: Synthesis Report for the EMN Focussed Study 2015." European Migration Network, Brussels.

Felbermayr, Gabriel J., Sanne Hiller, and Davide Sala. 2010. "Does Immigration Boost Per Capita Income?" *Economics Letters* 107 (2): 177–79.

Hansen, Marianne Frank, Marie Louise Schultz-Nielsen, and Torben Tranæs. 2017. "The Fiscal Impact of Immigration to Welfare States of the Scandinavian Type." *Journal of Population Economics* 30 (3): 925–52.

Hunt, Jennifer, and Marjolaine Gauthier-Loiselle. 2010. "How Much Does Immigration Boost Innovation?" *American Economic Journal: Macroeconomics* 2 (2): 31–56.

Jaumotte, Florence, Ksenia Koloskova, and Sweta Chaman Saxena. 2016. "Impact of Migration on Income Levels in Advanced Economies." IMF Spillover Note 8, International Monetary Fund, Washington, DC.

Kang, Youngho, and Byung-Yeon Kim. 2012. "Immigration and Economic Growth: Do Origin and Destination Matter?" CEI Working Paper 2012-01, Center for Economic Institutions, Institute of Economic Research, Hitotsubashi University, Tokyo.

Lodigiani, Elisabetta. 2008. "Diaspora Externalities and Technology Diffusion." *Économie Internationale* 3 (115): 43–64.

Longhi, Simonetta, Peter Nijkamp, and Jacques Poot. 2005. "A Meta-Analytic Assessment of the Effect of Immigration on Wages." *Journal of Economic Surveys* 19 (3): 451–77.

Lutz, Wolfgang, Anne Goujon, Samir KC, Marcin Stonawski, and Nikolaos Stilianakis, eds. 2018. *Demographic and Human Capital Scenarios for the 21st Century: 2018 Assessment for 201 Countries.* Luxembourg: Publications Office of the European Union.

Mitaritonna, Cristina, Gianluca Orefice, and Giovanni Peri. 2017. "Immigrants and Firms' Outcomes: Evidence from France." *European Economic Review* 96 (July): 62–82.

Muysken, Joan, and Thomas H. W. Ziesemer. 2011. "The Effect of Net Immigration on Economic Growth in an Ageing Economy: Transitory and Permanent Shocks." UNU-MERIT Working Paper 2011-055, United Nations University–Maastricht Economic and Social Research Institute on Innovation and Technology, Maastricht.

OECD (Organisation for Economic Co-operation and Development). 2013. "The Fiscal Impact of Immigration in OECD Countries." *International Migration Outlook 2013*, 125–89. Paris: OECD Publishing.

Orefice, Gianluca. 2010. "Skilled Migration and Economic Performances: Evidence from OECD Countries." Discussion Paper 2010-15, Institut de Recherches Economiques et Sociales, Université Catholique de Louvain, Louvain-la-Neuve, Belgium.

Ortega, Francesc, and Giovanni Peri. 2009. "The Causes and Effects of International Migrations: Evidence from OECD Countries 1980–2005." NBER Working Paper 14833, National Bureau of Economic Research, Cambridge, MA.

Ortega, Francesc, and Giovanni Peri. 2014. "The Aggregate Effects of Trade and Migration: Evidence from OECD Countries." In *The Socio-Economic Impact of Migration Flows: Effects Trade, Remittances, Output, and the Labour Market*, edited by Andrés Artal-Tur, Giovanni Peri, and Francisco Requena-Silvente, 19–52. Population Economics Series. London: Springer International Publishing.

Ottaviano, Gianmarco I. P., and Giovanni Peri. 2012. "Rethinking the Effect of Immigration on Wages." *Journal of the European Economic Association* 10 (1): 152–97.

Ottaviano, Gianmarco I. P., Giovanni Peri, and Greg C. Wright. 2018. "Immigration, Trade, and Productivity in Services: Evidence from U.K. Firms." *Journal of International Economics* 112 (May): 88–108.

Peri, Giovanni. 2012. "The Effect of Immigration on Productivity: Evidence from US States." *Review of Economics and Statistics* 94 (1): 348–58.

Peri, Giovanni. 2014. "Do Immigrant Workers Depress the Wages of Native Workers?" IZA World of Labor 42, Institute of Labor Economics, Bonn, Germany.

Peri, Giovanni, and Chad Sparber. 2009. "Task Specialization, Immigration, and Wages." *American Economic Journal: Applied Economics* 1 (3): 135–69.

Rowthorn, Robert. 2008. "The Fiscal Impact of Immigration on the Advanced Economies." *Oxford Review of Economic Policy* 24 (3): 560–80.

Rutledge, Zach, and Tim Kane. 2018. "Immigration and Economic Performance in the US: Evidence from the 50 States." Presentation at the 2018 Agricultural and Applied Economics Association's Annual Meeting, Washington, DC, August 5–7.

Trax, Michaela, Stephan Brunow, and Jens Suedekum. 2015. "Cultural Diversity and Plant-Level Productivity." *Regional Science and Urban Economics* 53 (July): 85–96.

Vandenbussche, Jérôme, Philippe Aghion, and Costas Meghir. 2006. "Growth, Distance to Frontier, and Composition of Human Capital." *Journal of Economic Growth* 11 (2): 97–127.

Vargas-Silva, Carlos. 2016. "EU Migration to and from the UK after Brexit." *Intereconomics* 51: 251–55.

World Bank. 2018. *Moving for Prosperity: Global Migration and Labor Markets*. Washington, DC: World Bank.

World Bank. 2019. "Migration and Brain Drain." Europe and Central Asia Economic Update, Office of the Chief Economist, World Bank, Washington, DC.

Zaiceva, Anzelika, and Klaus F. Zimmermann. 2008. "Scale, Diversity, and Determinants of Labour Migration in Europe." *Oxford Review of Economic Policy* 24 (3): 427–51.

5 The Impact of Migration on Sending Countries and Regions

SHORT-TERM COSTS IN HUMAN CAPITAL, REGIONAL INEQUALITY, AND FISCAL BALANCES

In the short run, emigration from sending countries can lead to slower capital growth and a technological downgrade. In the presence of skill complementarities or externalities between high-skilled workers in a firm, the emigration of some workers may negatively affect productivity among the stayers. The emigration of high-skilled migrants tends to harm, on average, domestic knowledge access, but it allows innovators at home to access valuable knowledge accumulated abroad (Agrawal et al. 2011). Some studies on European countries find negative effects of youth emigration on entrepreneurship and innovation in Italy (Anelli et al. 2019) and on firm productivity and total factor productivity in Eastern European countries (Giesing and Laurentsyeva 2017).

Already occurring because of aging and low fertility rates, population and labor force declines in the European Union (EU) are reinforced by emigration. Migration to the EU15 has exacerbated the natural drop in populations in Eastern Europe.[1] During the last two decades, net emigration flows have accounted for more than half the total decline in population in the 13 New Member States (NMS13) joining since 2004 (figure 5.1, panel a).[2] The role of migration outflows has been particularly significant in Lithuania and Romania; whereas in Bulgaria, Croatia, and Latvia, the declining fertility rate is the most relevant driver of population change. Migration thus seems to be amplifying unequal population trends within the EU.

Migration also reinforces rapid aging among the populations of migrant-sending countries. Because younger people show greater tendency to migrate, old-age dependency ratios have risen more quickly among countries exhibiting larger migrant outflows than among countries showing larger migrant inflows (figure 5.1, panel b). Intra-EU mobility, which accounts for a large part of EU immigration, cannot address the overall EU aging issue. In contrast, it tends to exacerbate the challenge in some countries, especially in Eastern European migrant-sending countries.

FIGURE 5.1

Population change and aging, migrant-sending regions of the European Union, 1995–2017

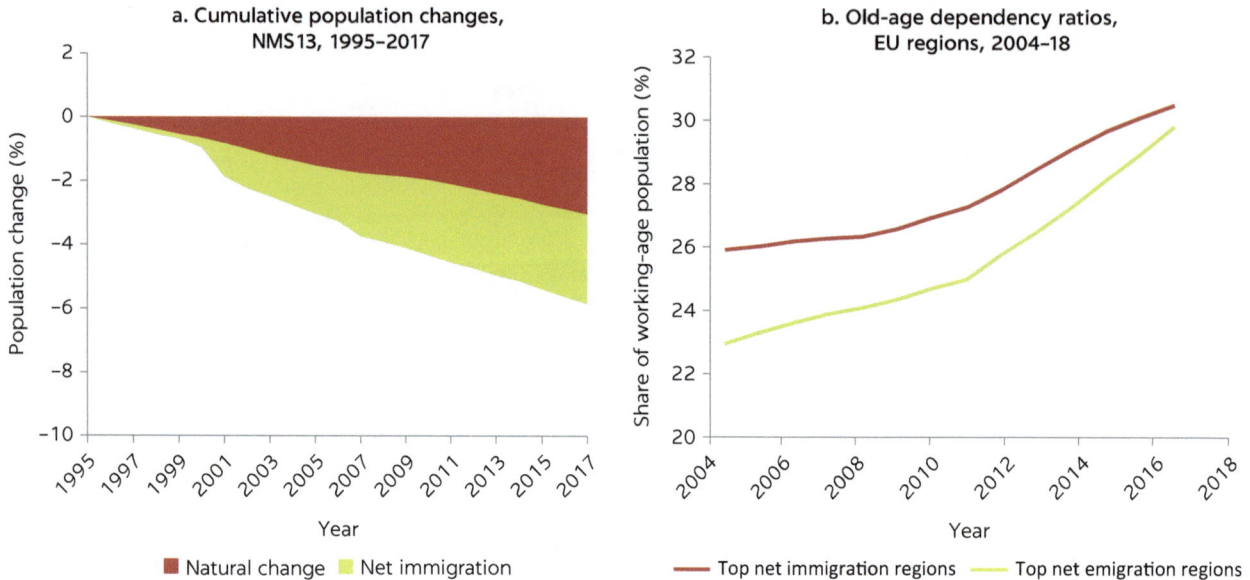

a. Cumulative population changes, NMS13, 1995–2017

b. Old-age dependency ratios, EU regions, 2004–18

■ Natural change ■ Net immigration

— Top net immigration regions — Top net emigration regions

Source: Population (database), Eurostat, European Commission, https://ec.europa.eu/eurostat/web/population/overview.
Note: Net immigration is defined as the difference between immigration flows (arrivals) and emigration flows (departures) in a given European region. For panel b, the Nomenclature of Territorial Units for Statistics (NUTS) classification system is a geocode standard for referencing the subdivisions of countries for statistical purposes. The highly aggregated NUTS 2 second-level subdivisions are used in EU regional programs and policy making. Top net immigration (emigration) areas are the 30 percent of total EU NUTS 2 subdivisions with larger net inflows (outflows). EU = European Union; NMS13 = New Member States joining in 2004, 2007, and 2013 (Bulgaria, Croatia, Cyprus, the Czech Republic, Estonia, Hungary, Latvia, Lithuania, Malta, Poland, Romania, the Slovak Republic, and Slovenia).

The emigration of a segment of the high-skilled population reduces the average level of human capital in a country in the short run. Emigrants in the EU generally exhibit greater educational attainment relative to nonmigrants who remain in the home country (figure 5.2). Those who migrate also tend to be in occupations with more transferable skills, such as those in science, technology, engineering, and mathematics. This trend is observed across both western EU countries and the NMS13. Only in Portugal is the share of adults with tertiary educational attainment lower among emigrants than among stayers. In the NMS13, adults with low or tertiary educational attainment are more likely than adults with midlevel skills to emigrate. Since the accession of the NMS13 to the EU in 2004, there has been a positive correlation between net immigration flows and changes in tertiary educational attainment in EU Nomenclature of Territorial Units for Statistics 2 (NUTS 2) regions (see figure 4.2 in chapter 4). Migrant-sending regions in the EU have thereby lagged in human capital accumulation compared with more vibrant areas.

Emigration affects critical sectors, such as health care, potentially causing shortages of qualified professionals in the EU15 south and in the NMS13. Annual flows of doctors from the EU15 south and the NMS13 to the EU15 north and European Free Trade Association (EFTA) countries have been large (figure 5.3).[3] Annual inflows from other EU and EFTA countries have been especially large in Ireland, Luxembourg, Norway, and Switzerland, representing between 3 percent and 9 percent of the total stock of physicians in these countries in 2007–18. Migration outflows of doctors have been more prevalent in some southern EU15 countries and the NMS13, particularly Estonia and Romania, averaging

FIGURE 5.2

Tertiary educational attainment, age 25–64, by emigration status, European Union

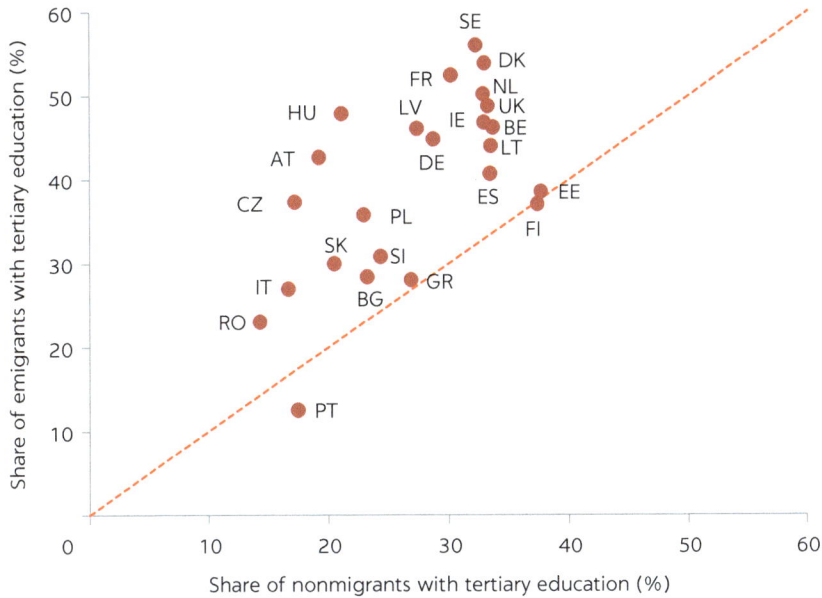

Source: DIOC (Database on Immigrants in OECD and Non-OECD Countries), reference years 2010/11, Organisation for Economic Co-operation and Development, Paris, https://www.oecd.org/els/mig/dioc.htm.

FIGURE 5.3

Average annual migration flows among doctors, EU and EFTA, 2007–18

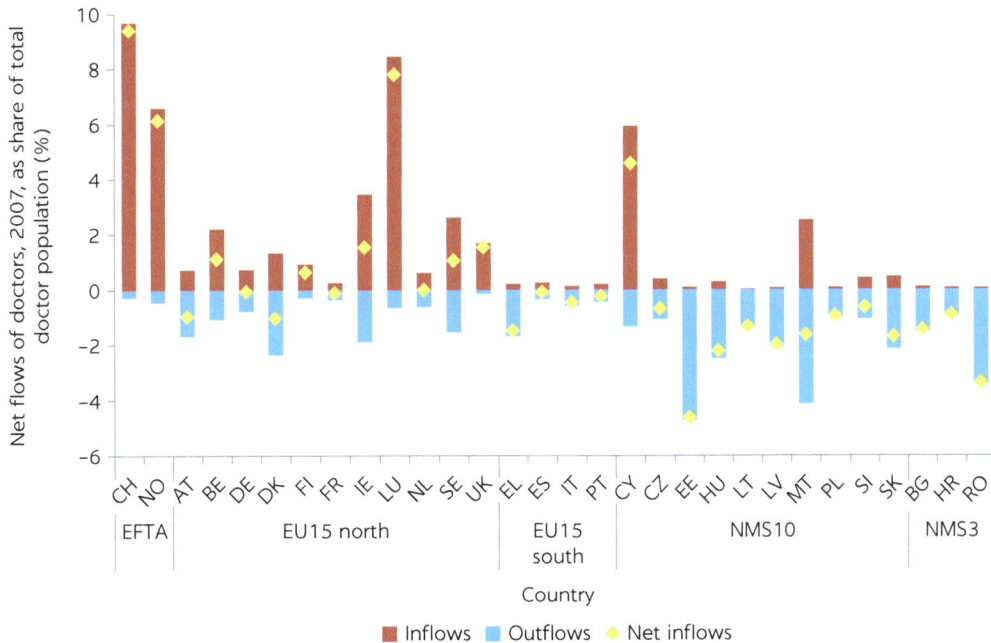

Source: Elaboration based on data from the Regulated Professions Database, European Commission, Brussels, https://ec.europa.eu/growth/tools-databases/regprof/index.cfm?action=homepage.
Note: The EU15 north includes all the EU15, with the exception of Greece, Italy, Portugal, and Spain, which represent the EU15 south. EFTA = European Free Trade Association; EU15 = European Union members before 2004; NMS10 = New Member States that completed formal EU accession in 2004; NMS3 = New Member States that completed formal EU accession in 2007 (Bulgaria and Romania) or 2013 (Croatia).

3.9 percent and 2.5 percent annually, respectively, during the same period. The potential reduction in the stock of health professionals should be monitored, given the essential role of health professionals in socioeconomic outcomes among the population.

Outflows of doctors from the NMS13 and the EU15 south have been sizable during the last decade, reaching, respectively, 0.7 percent and 1.5 percent of the total stock of physicians in these regions by 2014 (figure 5.4). These substantial outflows of doctors were largely absorbed by the EU15 north and EFTA countries. While the migration of health professionals has stabilized or even slowed in recent years, it still accounts for a sizable portion of the domestic supply of these professionals.

Even in countries where emigration has been widespread, the effects on the wages of natives at origin have been limited. In sending countries in Eastern Europe such as Lithuania (Elsner 2013) or Poland (Dustman, Frattini, and Rosso 2015), emigration was found to have a positive effect on wages of workers in the home country who have skills similar to those of the workers who emigrate, because of reduced competition. Also, emigration has been found to have negative effects on the wages of less educated native workers who have skills that are complementary to those of high-skilled emigrants (Docquier, Özden, and Peri 2014; Dustmann, Frattini, and Rosso 2015). However, the two other forces at play in equilibrium wages—native population aging and upskilling—have more than compensated for the negative effects of emigration on the wages of natives in migrant-sending countries (Docquier et al. 2018).

FIGURE 5.4

Inflows and outflows of migrant doctors, EU15 and NMS13, 2007–18

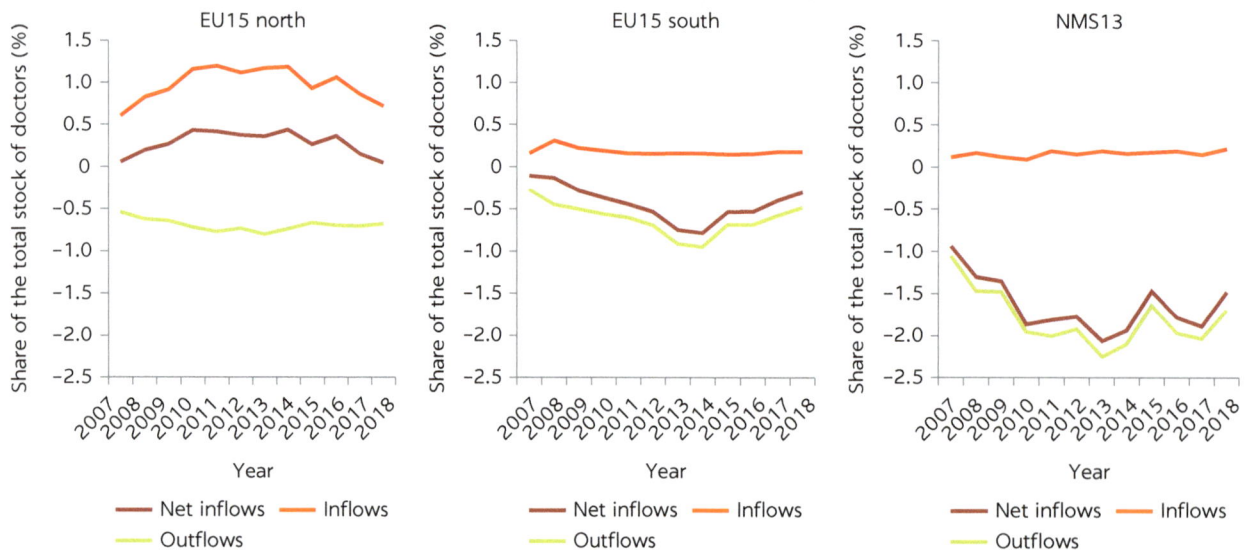

Source: Elaboration based on data from the Regulated Professions Database, European Commission, Brussels, https://ec.europa.eu/growth /tools-databases/regprof/index.cfm?action=homepage.
Note: The EU15 north includes all the EU15, with the exception of Greece, Italy, Portugal, and Spain, which represent the EU15 south. EU15 = European Union members before 2004 (Austria, Belgium, Denmark, Finland, France, Germany, Greece, Ireland, Italy, Luxembourg, the Netherlands, Portugal, Spain, Sweden, and the United Kingdom); NMS13 = New Member States joining in 2004, 2007, and 2013 (Bulgaria, Croatia, Cyprus, the Czech Republic, Estonia, Hungary, Latvia, Lithuania, Malta, Poland, Romania, the Slovak Republic, and Slovenia).

In the short run, emigration reduces the fiscal base and can negatively affect public finances. Tax revenues may be reduced as a result of the lower economic activity due to labor outflows (Gibson and McKenzie 2012), although remittances can raise consumption taxes, thereby exerting a mitigating impact. On the expenditure side, the older population left behind puts pressure on pension and health spending (Clements et al. 2015). Fiscal losses become larger if emigrants are concentrated among prime-age, highly educated, and high-earning workers (Desai et al. 2009). In the NMS13, net immigration has been associated with higher social spending on pensions and health care during periods of weaker economic growth (Atoyan et al. 2016). The reduction of the fiscal base is especially a problem in education because nonmigrants subsidize those who leave.

Sending regions lag along several dimensions, including human capital. Educational attainment among the adult population in the EU has progressively increased since the EU's enlargement in 2004. Among the NMS13, there has been a process of catching up to the EU15, which is more visible in the younger population age 30–34 years (figure 5.5). However, the top migrant-sending regions among the NMS13 have been slower to improve. They have not reached the EU15 average and have experienced larger gaps relative to the average among populations in the NMS13. Migration in NMS sending regions, which usually involves more highly educated populations, seems to slow the convergence in human capital across these regions.

FIGURE 5.5

Tertiary education, age 30–34, EU regions sending or receiving migrants, 2004–18

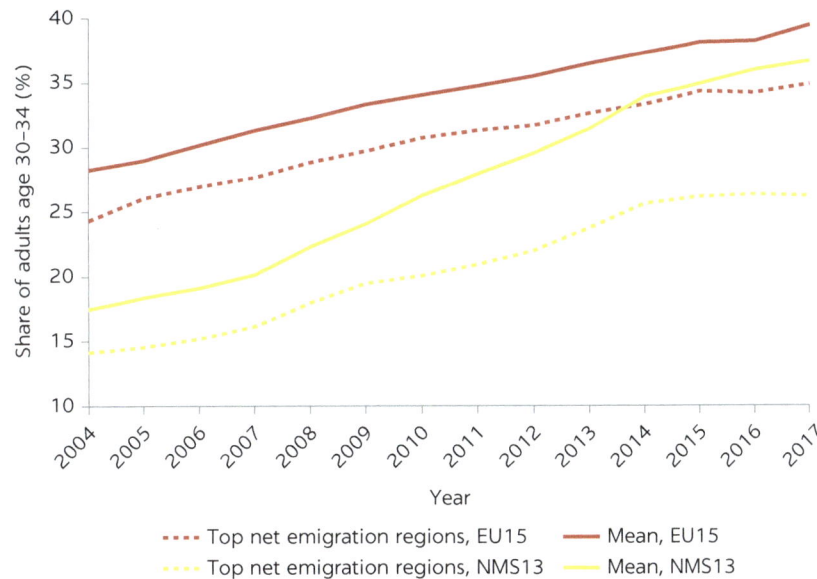

Source: Elaboration based on data from Education and Training (database), Eurostat, European Commission, Luxembourg, https://ec.europa.eu/eurostat/web/education-and -training/overview.
Note: Top net emigration regions are the 30 percent of total EU15 and NMS13 NUTS 2 subdivisions with the largest net outflows of migrants. EU15 = European Union members before 2004 (Austria, Belgium, Denmark, Finland, France, Germany, Greece, Ireland, Italy, Luxembourg, the Netherlands, Portugal, Spain, Sweden, and the United Kingdom); NMS13 = New Member States joining in 2004, 2007, and 2013 (Bulgaria, Croatia, Cyprus, the Czech Republic, Estonia, Hungary, Latvia, Lithuania, Malta, Poland, Romania, the Slovak Republic, and Slovenia). NUTS 2 = Nomenclature of Territorial Units for Statistics 2.

MEDIUM-TERM EFFECTS ON LABOR SUPPLY, HUMAN CAPITAL ACCUMULATION, AND REMITTANCES

Migration may support a more efficient relocation of labor market factors and alleviate unemployment pressures in sending regions with scant job opportunities, especially among youth. Before the 2008–09 global financial crisis, migration from high- to low-unemployment areas coincided with a substantial decline in unemployment in the top migrant-sending countries (figure 5.6). However, this convergence may have been driven by other economic factors associated with EU enlargement. This appears to be the case because the average unemployment rate fell more rapidly in the NMS13 than in the top migrant-sending countries. The 2008–09 crisis affected all EU countries, putting on hold the convergence across regions. Beyond the extensive margin of employment, migration also allows skilled labor to be reallocated from low- to high-productivity regions and sectors, with potential benefits for migrants and the economy.

Emigration can incentivize human capital investment in response to increasing external and internal demand. In addition to the immediate short-term drain on human capital associated with emigration, the departure of skilled workers can also lead in the long run to what has been referred to as a brain gain in

FIGURE 5.6

Unemployment rates, by NUTS 2 regions, 2004–17

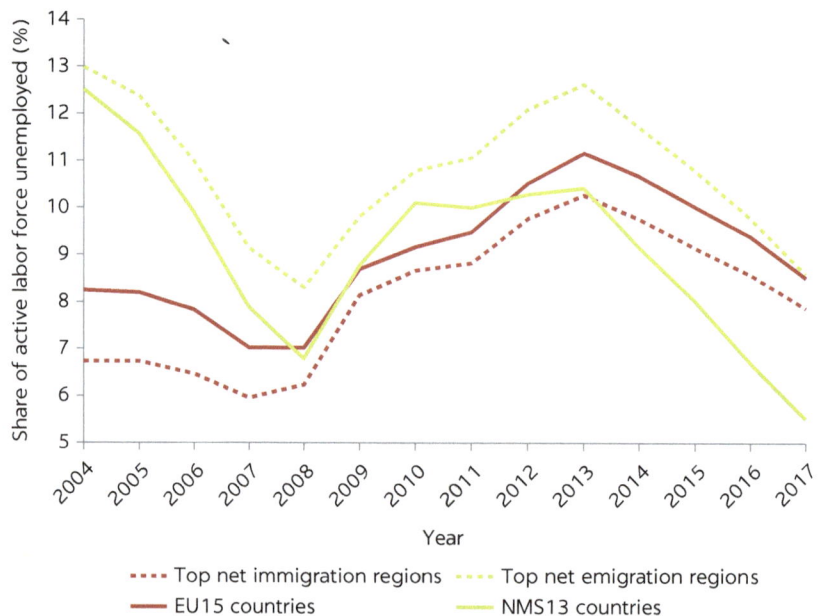

Sources: Estimates based on data from the European Union Labour Force Survey (database), Eurostat, European Commission, Luxembourg, https://ec.europa.eu/eurostat /statistics-explained/index.php/EU_labour_force_survey; Population (database), Eurostat, European Commission, Luxembourg, https://ec.europa.eu/eurostat/web/population /overview.
Note: Top net immigration (emigration) areas are the top 30 percent of NUTS 2 country administrative subdivisions with the highest migrant inflows minus outflows (outflows minus inflows) during 2004–17. EU15 = European Union members before 2004 (Austria, Belgium, Denmark, Finland, France, Germany, Greece, Ireland, Italy, Luxembourg, the Netherlands, Portugal, Spain, Sweden, and the United Kingdom); NMS13 = New Member States joining in 2004, 2007, and 2013 (Bulgaria, Croatia, Cyprus, the Czech Republic, Estonia, Hungary, Latvia, Lithuania, Malta, Poland, Romania, the Slovak Republic, and Slovenia); NUTS 2 = Nomenclature of Territorial Units for Statistics 2.

migrant-sending countries. The more recent literature has emphasized many indirect, longer-run feedback channels through which skilled emigration positively affects human capital growth in migrant-sending countries. Most cross-country studies that include sending countries in Europe find a positive association between emigration and human capital accumulation at origin in the long run. Beine, Docquier, and Rapoport (2008) find a positive effect of skilled migration prospects on gross (premigration) human capital levels in a cross-section of 127 developing countries. Using a cross-sectional analysis in a sample of sending countries, Beine, Defoort, and Docquier (2011) and Docquier and Rapoport (2009) also find robust, positive, and sizable effects of skilled migration prospects on human capital formation in developing countries. Among sending countries in Eastern Europe, return migration, combined with the education incentive channel, has been shown to turn the drain on human capital into a brain gain in 10 migrant-sending countries in Eastern Europe (Beine, Docquier, and Rapoport 2001, 2008; Mayr and Peri 2009; Docquier and Rapoport 2012). In a panel regression of the 10 countries that joined the EU in 2004, plus Greece, Portugal, and Spain, who joined the EU in the 1980s, Farchy (2009) also finds evidence in support of the brain gain hypothesis as human capital expands as a result of the increased mobility derived from the EU accession. In Romania specifically, temporary emigration was found to have positive long-run effects on skill levels at home (Ambrosini et al. 2015).

One key mechanism through which brain gain takes place is the increase in the returns to education in home countries because of the demand for skilled migrants by destination countries. Recent empirical studies of brain gain outside Eastern Europe that are relevant for that region offer evidence of the indirect, endogenous effects of emigration on human capital in sending countries. Abarcar and Theoharides (2018) find that an increase in the migration of nurses leads to a rise in the number of nurses in the sending country, enabled by the increase in both the local demand for nursing programs and the domestic supply of nursing programs. Similarly, the direct effect of the emigration of doctors, which reduces the stock of doctors in sending countries, may eventually be offset because of the greater incentives to graduate in medicine due to higher earnings potential abroad and the option value of returning with enhanced skills after several years of work abroad.

Several conditions need to be fulfilled, however, for brain gain to occur. First, brain gain occurs only if a large enough number of newly educated individuals do not migrate overseas or if they ultimately return to sending countries. Second, the home country of the migrants should be able to increase school capacity, meeting increased demand for education. For example, although the size of the cohort of new graduates in medicine was close to constant in the northern EU15 countries between 2004 and 2016, the number of new graduates in medicine showed an upward trend in the NMS13, especially during the first five or six years after EU accession (figure 5.7). In the NMS10,[4] which completed formal EU accession in 2004, the size of the cohort of graduates in medicine accelerated in 2009; in the NMS3, which entered the EU in 2007 (Bulgaria and Romania) and 2013 (Croatia), graduate flows accelerated beginning in 2013. Box 5.1 elaborates on the effects of emigration of doctors on human capital accumulation in Romania.

Education capacity must expand to accommodate the increased demand, which has not occurred in all NMS13 countries; and when it does, it has an additional fiscal cost for sending countries. Because the net outflows of doctors rose in all NMS13 countries following EU accession, the net changes in the stock of physicians were dependent on changes in the supply of new cohorts of doctors.

FIGURE 5.7

New graduates in medicine, NMS10 and NMS3, 2004–16

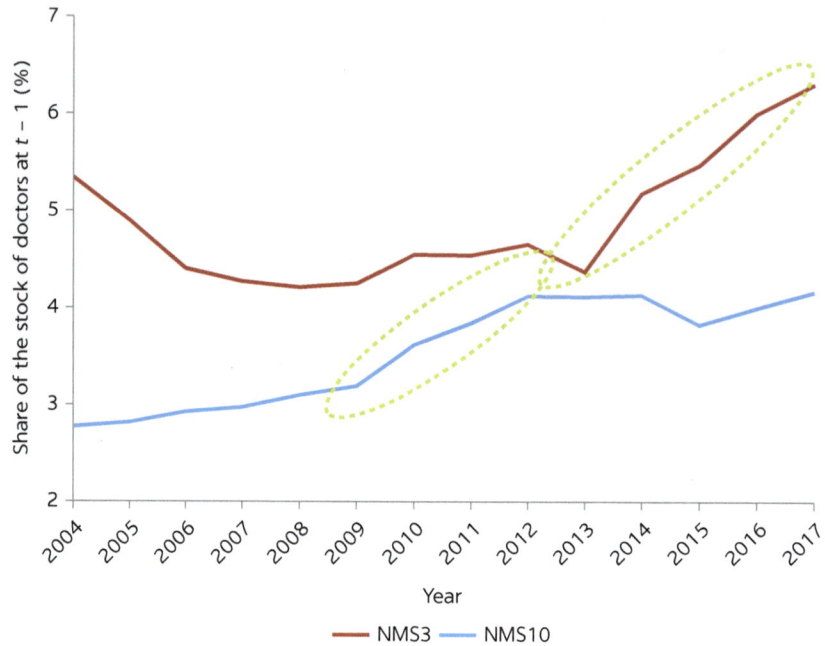

Source: Elaboration based on data from the Regulated Professions Database, European Commission, Brussels, https://ec.europa.eu/growth/tools-databases/regprof/index .cfm?action=homepage.
Note: The dotted ovals highlight the increase in the share of doctors 5–6 years after the EU accession, which is the number of years required to complete medical school. NMS10 = New Member States that completed formal EU accession in 2004 (Cyprus, the Czech Republic, Estonia, Hungary, Latvia, Lithuania, Malta, Poland, the Slovak Republic, and Slovenia); NMS3 = New Member States that completed formal EU accession in 2007 (Bulgaria and Romania) or 2013 (Croatia).

Box 5.1

Emigration of high-skilled professionals from Romania

Romania is the second-largest emigration country in the European Union (EU) after Poland. Approximately 3.5 million Romanians live abroad, of whom 90 percent reside in other EU countries.[a] Emigration accelerated after Romania's accession to the EU in 2007 and displays large regional disparities. Whereas the largest urban centers with higher concentrations of high-quality jobs (such as Bucharest, Cluj, and Timis) have recorded net migration inflows since 2002, lagging counties have faced large emigration flows.

Following similar patterns as other New Member States of the EU, Romanian emigrants are much younger, on average, than the population remaining in Romania, reinforcing the country's aging phenomenon.

Romanian emigrants are also more educated than the general population of Romania. In 2011, the latest year for which data are available, about one in four Romanian emigrants aged 25–64 years had completed tertiary education, compared to only 13 percent of Romanians who stayed in the country.

The large emigration of qualified professionals has raised worries about emerging shortages across key occupations. Among them, shortages of doctors are of particular concern, given the large outflows observed since 2007 and their essential role for the well-being of the population. According to the Ministry of Health, 43,000 doctors emigrated between 2007 and 2017. As a result, labor shortages—measured by the share of job vacancies over employment—increased

continued

Box 5.1, *continued*

between 2013 and 2018 most rapidly in the health and social work sector.[b]

Despite those worries, the opportunity to emigrate and obtain larger economic returns has incentivized more Romanians to study medicine. The number of graduates in medicine in Romania has increased since its EU accession in 2007 and accelerated six years after that, in line with the time that it takes to complete medical school programs (figure B5.1.1, panel a). Although other factors might be at play, the fact that most of the increase in medical graduates stems from programs in English and French also points at the higher demand for internationally transferable skills.[c] Because of emigration, the increasing supply of medical graduates might not always translate into a larger stock of doctors in Romania; however, Eurostat statistics show a 58 percent increase in the number of

physicians per capita in Romania between 2000 and 2018 (figure B5.1.1, panel b). Emigration, thus, does not seem to have hampered the process of catching up with other countries, with the ratio of doctors vis-à-vis the EU average increasing from 66 percent in 2000 to 82 percent in 2018. Although the aging of Romania's population has increased the demand for doctors, the supply has risen about 14 percent since 2000 as a proportion of the population above 65 years old.

Although there is no evidence of migration causing a reduction in the stock of doctors in Romania, several challenges have emerged. First, financing the education of medical students who emigrate is costly, particularly if they do not return to work in Romania. Second, up to now, Romania has shown little ability to attract Romanian emigrant doctors back to the country (Roman and Goschin 2014), given the

FIGURE B5.1.1

Trends in the supply of medical students and the stock of doctors in Romania, 2000–18

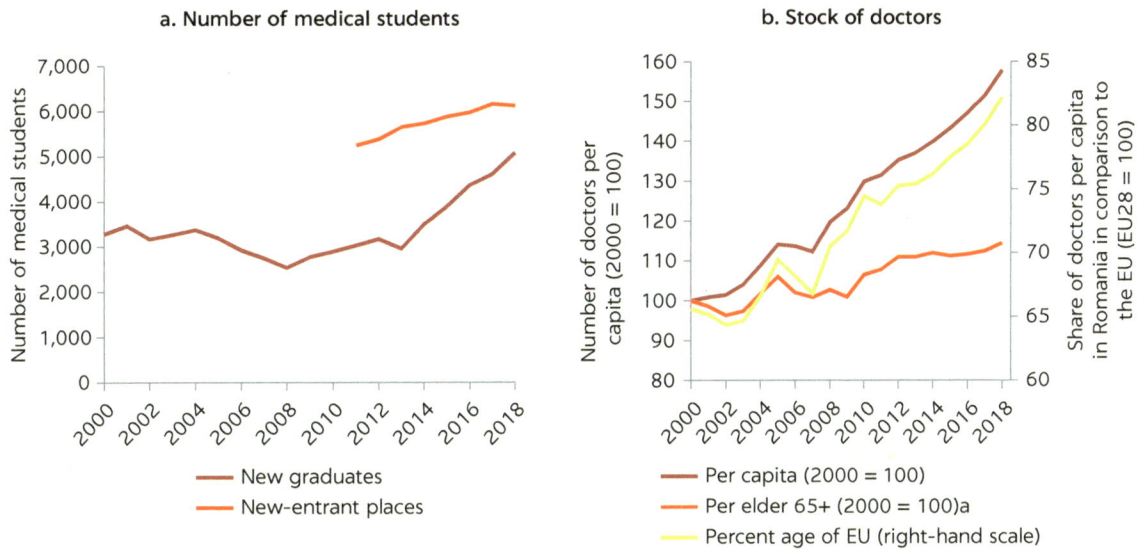

a. Number of medical students

b. Stock of doctors

Sources: Health graduates: Eurostat, European Commission, Luxembourg, https://appsso.eurostat.ec.europa.eu/nui/show.do?dataset=hlth_rs_grd&lang=en. Stock of doctors: Health personnel by NUTS 2 regions [hlth_rs_prsrg], Eurostat, European Commission, Luxembourg, https://ec.europa.eu/eurostat/en/web/products-datasets/-/HLTH_RS_PRSRG. New-entrant places: Organisation for Economic Co-operation and Development, Paris, https://www.oecd-ilibrary.org/sites/7db45b20-en/index.html?itemId=/content/component/7db45b20-en. Population: Population (database), Eurostat, European Commission, Luxembourg, reference years 2013/18, Population on January 1, by age group and sex [demo_pjangroup], https://ec.europa.eu/eurostat/web/population/overview.

Note: New-entrant places refers to the number of students that start studying medicine. EU = European Union; EU28 = full EU membership before the departure of the United Kingdom in 2020 (Brexit); NUTS 2 = Nomenclature of Territorial Units for Statistics 2.

continued

Box 5.1, *continued*

large wage differentials. Finally, the brain drain of doctors might be more of a concern in certain lagging regions. According to census data for 2011, there is a strong negative correlation between net emigration in each of the 42 counties and the observed increases in the stock of doctors. Because net emigration is correlated with the level of income per capita in a region, migration can amplify regional inequalities in the availability of qualified medical professionals in Romania.

a. Estimates vary, from 3.4 million in 2018 according to the OECD International Migration Database to the 3.6 million projected in 2019 by UN Department of Economic and Social Affairs population statistics.
b. Based on data from the Romanian National Institute of Statistics.
c. This pattern is also due to government efforts to internationalize medical education in Romania to attract foreign students offering diplomas recognized across the EU at lower tuition and living costs.

The Czech Republic, Romania, and Slovenia witnessed a rapid rise in the number of graduates in medicine that more than compensated for the out-migration of doctors; however, in Estonia, Hungary, and Latvia, the additional supply of new graduates was not sufficient to compensate for the drain on human resources (see figure 5.8 for the examples of Hungary and Romania). Even if migration can incentivize human capital accumulation, it still does not solve the problem of sending countries bearing the costs to educate that part of the population that leaves the country and thus does not give back to the local economy.

Overall, because of rapid aging, the supply of doctors in the NMS13 has not caught up with demand. Despite the migration of doctors from the NMS13 and the EU15 south to the EU15 north and EFTA countries, the overall supply of doctors has been rising progressively in all subregions since 2007 (figure 5.9, panel a). The stock of doctors has grown most rapidly in the NMS3, which represents the newest EU members (Bulgaria, Croatia, and Romania). In 10 years, the stock of doctors increased by about 29 percent, compared with 14 percent in the EU15 north and 9 percent in both the EU15 south and the rest of the NMS13. Given rapid aging in the EU, however, the region is likely to face a general rise in the demand for health care professionals. The number of doctors measured against the size of the older population (age 65 and older) can approximate these demand pressures more closely. By such a measure, the share of doctors in the EU15 has dropped by 3.7 percent since 2011, from 1,982 doctors to 1,909 doctors per 100,000 elderly population (figure 5.9, panel b). This shortage may represent a pull factor that attracts doctors and other health care professionals from elsewhere in Europe. In the NMS13, the ratio of doctors per 100,000 elderly population has fallen more, by over 13 percent since the 2004 EU accession and by 8 percent since 2011. Thus, although the stock of doctors in the NMS has risen despite the migration outflows to higher-income European countries, the expansion in supply has not kept up with the rapid aging of the population and the consequent increase in the demand for health care services.

Understanding why the supply of education responds more effectively in some NMS13 countries than in others to high-skilled emigration is important for policy making. For instance, some countries may have rigid training systems for particular occupations—such as highly regulated systems based on narrow entry criteria or a small, fixed number of places in medical education—that are not necessarily aligned with the needs created by changes in internal or international demand for

FIGURE 5.8

Changes in the stock of doctors, Hungary and Romania, 2000–17

a. Hungary

b. Romania

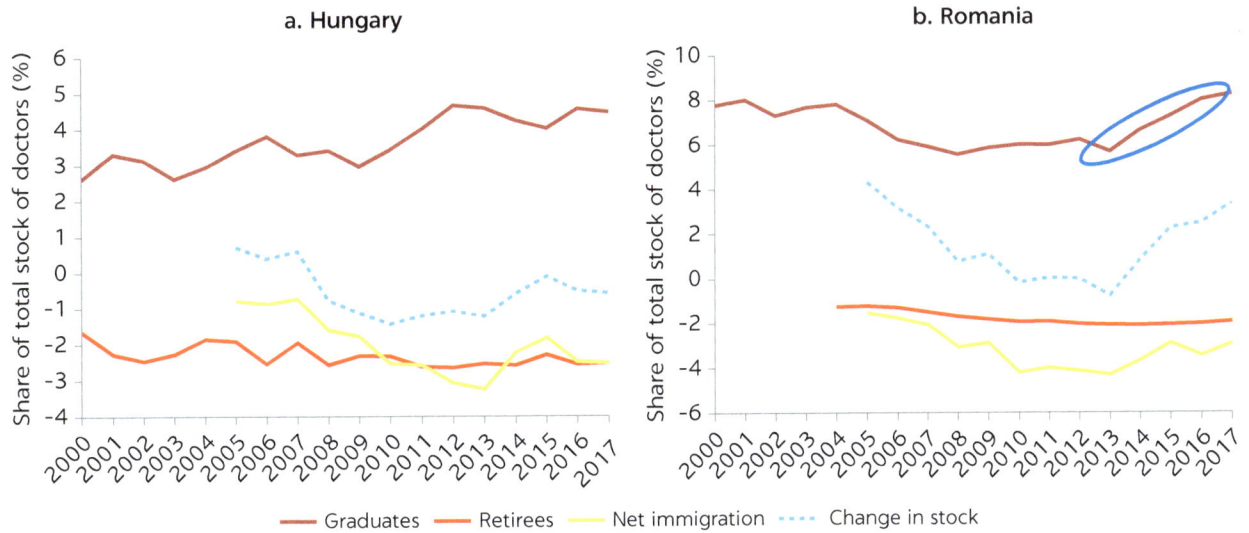

— Graduates   — Retirees   — Net immigration   ---- Change in stock

Source: Elaboration based on data of the Regulated Professions Database, European Commission, Brussels, https://ec.europa.eu/growth /tools-databases/regprof/index.cfm?action=homepage.
Note: Net immigration is defined as the difference between immigration flows (arrivals) and emigration flows (departures) in a given European region. The blue oval in panel b highlights the increase in the number of new graduates as a share of the total stock of doctors six years after Romania's accession to the European Union.

FIGURE 5.9

The stock of doctors as an index and per 100,000 population age 65 and older

a. Index of the stock of doctors, 2007–17

b. Doctors per 100,000 population age 65+, 2001–17

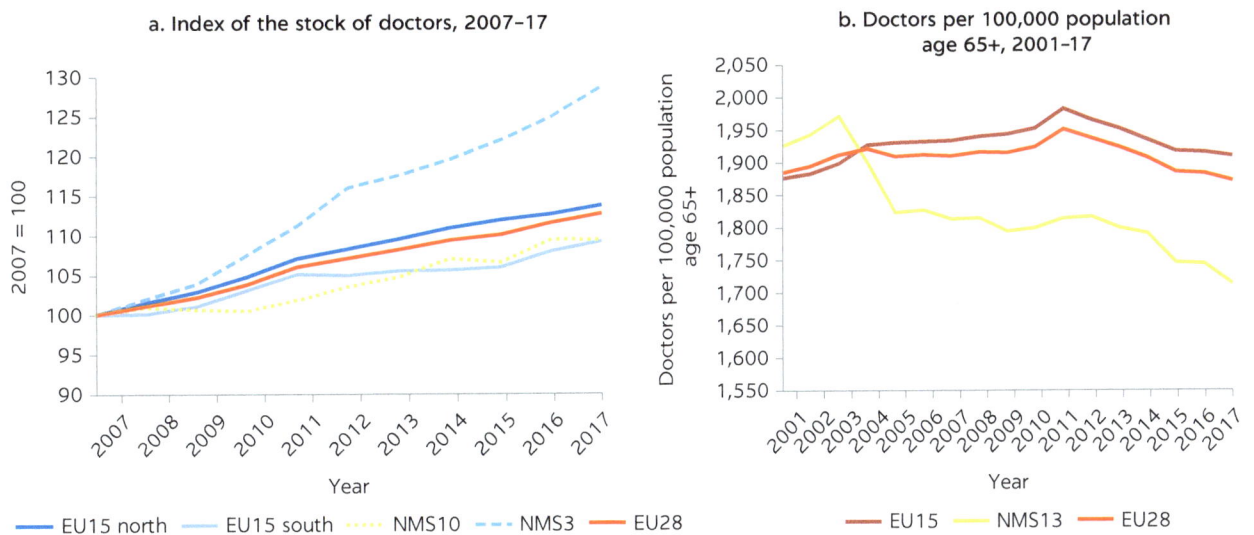

— EU15 north   — EU15 south   ···· NMS10   --- NMS3   — EU28

— EU15   — NMS13   — EU28

Source: Elaboration based on data of the Regulated Professions Database, European Commission, Brussels, https://ec.europa.eu/growth /tools-databases/regprof/index.cfm?action=homepage.
Note: EU15 = European Union members before 2004; EU15 north = Austria, Belgium, Denmark, Finland, France, Germany, Ireland, Luxembourg, the Netherlands, Sweden, and the United Kingdom; EU15 south = Greece, Italy, Portugal, and Spain; NMS3 = Bulgaria, Croatia, and Romania; NMS10 = Cyprus, the Czech Republic, Estonia, Hungary, Latvia, Lithuania, Malta, Poland, the Slovak Republic, and Slovenia; NMS13 = New Member States joining the EU in 2004 and after.

these occupations. These countries may thus be more likely to experience shortages locally than other countries in which there is no quota system or in which quotas may be readily adjusted to account for shifts in domestic demand.

In addition to the brain gain discussed earlier, another benefit of emigration for sending countries is the growth in remittances sent mainly to lower-income households. Since the mid-1990s, remittances have quadrupled in the NMS13 as a share of gross domestic product (from 0.5 percent in 1994 to above 2.0 percent in 2013–18) (figure 5.10). Remittances are particularly prevalent in Croatia, Bulgaria, and Latvia, where they represent 4.7, 3.7, and 3.6 percent of gross domestic product, respectively. Remittances provide vital income to many households, especially the poorest, and have been associated with better health and education outcomes and lower poverty rates (Adams and Page 2005; Amuedo-Dorantes and Pozo 2010; Hildebrandt and McKenzie 2005). For sending countries, remittance flows have a stabilizing effect on the economy and public finances because they tend to be countercyclical (Chami, Hakura, and Montiel 2009). This pattern might be less at play in the EU, given the coordination of the business cycle between countries in recent years. For example, remittances fell in most NMS13 countries during the financial and euro crises—given that most NMS13 migrants reside in EU15 countries—while their economies experienced a slowdown.

Remittances may, however, reduce labor supply at home among households with international migrants. Disposable income brought by remittances could dampen the incentives to work for nonmigrating family members, by raising the reservation wage of family members through an income effect. In that case, the increase in income from remittances may reduce the labor force participation of family members, and in the long term it may create dependency on income from remittances. Evidence on this topic for Europe is very scarce, but studies in other contexts typically find negative effects of having a migrant currently overseas on women's labor supply at home, whereas effects for men are quite small and

FIGURE 5.10

The share of remittances in gross domestic product, NMS13, 1994–2018

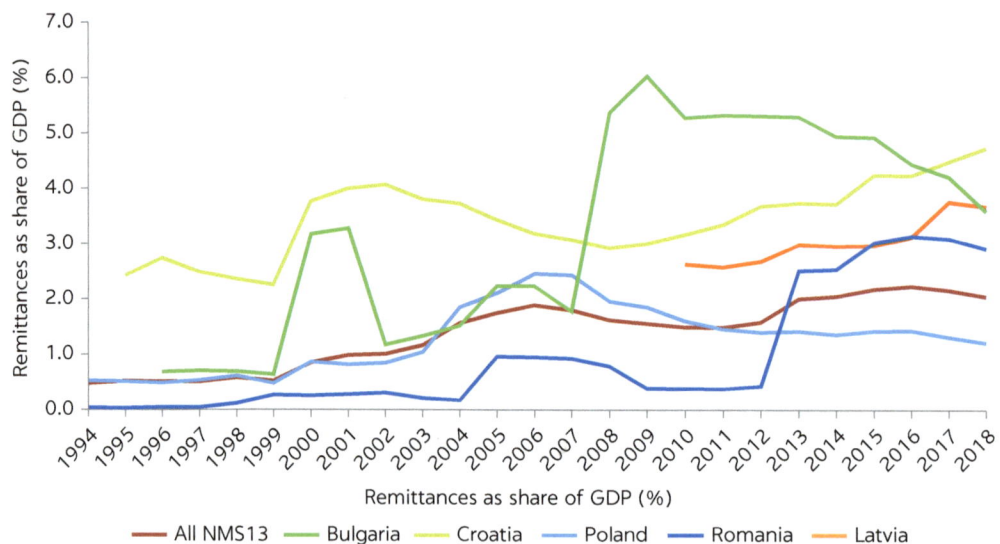

Source: Data from the World Development Indicators (database), World Bank, Washington, DC, http://data.worldbank.org/products/wdi.
Note: NMS13 = New Member States joining the European Union in 2004, 2007, and 2013 (Bulgaria, Croatia, Cyprus, the Czech Republic, Estonia, Hungary, Latvia, Lithuania, Malta, Poland, Romania, the Slovak Republic, and Slovenia).

ambiguous. In Albania, emigration was found to decrease female paid labor supply while increasing unpaid work (Mendola and Carletto 2012). In contrast, women with past family migration experience were significantly more likely to engage in self-employment and less likely to supply unpaid work.

LONG-TERM EFFECTS: IMPROVEMENTS IN INSTITUTIONS, TRADE, KNOWLEDGE, AND PRODUCTIVITY

In the longer run, emigration may contribute to improving institutions in migrant-sending countries. For example, migrants to more democratic societies can have a positive impact on social, economic, and political institutions at home (Docquier et al. 2011; Spilimbergo 2009). Because better institutions usually translate into higher total factor productivity, such institutional channels are partly captured by productivity responses. In Moldova, the emigration wave that started in the aftermath of the 1998 crisis in the Russian Federation strongly affected electoral outcomes and political preferences during the following decade, eventually contributing to the fall of the last Communist government in Europe (Barsbai et al. 2017).

Emigration can also reduce international transaction costs and generate global networks, promoting bilateral trade, foreign direct investment, and knowledge diffusion between the migrant's home and host countries. There is extensive evidence that emigrants, especially the highly skilled, keep a wide range of professional ties to their native countries (Saxenian 2002; Wescott and Brinkerhoff 2006). For example, there is a well-established model of cooperation between the Indian diaspora and Indian information technology service vendors (Pandey et al. 2006). Emigrants may also be catalysts for knowledge diffusion (Bahar and Rapoport 2018; Kerr 2008). The importance of diasporas in facilitating trade has been the focus of many recent studies from both the theoretical level (Greif 1993; Rauch and Casella 2003) and an empirical perspective (Genc et al. 2012; Gould 1994; Head and Ries 1998; Herander and Saavedra 2005; Orefice et al. 2021; Peri and Requena-Silvente 2010; Rauch and Trindade 2002). Business networks in home countries have been shown to be mostly driven by skilled migration (Docquier and Lodigiani 2010). Although high-skilled migration and foreign direct investment flows are negatively correlated contemporaneously, skilled migration is associated with future increases in foreign direct investment inflows due to the formation of business networks (Kugler and Rapoport 2007). As a result, transnational migrant networks enable the home regions of emigrants to integrate more quickly into the EU and the world economy.

High-skilled migration exhibits substantial circularity in the EU15, but the NMS13 countries struggle to encourage the return of skilled migrants. Many migrants initially plan to migrate for a short period or end up migrating for only a limited time, usually for specific purposes, such as temporary work or education. Dustmann and Weiss (2007) and Dustmann and Goerlach (2016) stress the relevance of temporary migration, whereby migrants return home after several years of working abroad, even in the continuing presence of wage differentials. They point to price differentials, complementarities of consumption and location where consumption takes place, and human capital obtained abroad that enhance immigrants' earnings potential at home as potential drivers of the decision to return. Return decisions are also affected by the labor market outcomes of migrants in destination countries, such as in the Netherlands (Bijward,

Schluter, and Wahba 2014). The decision to return of highly skilled migrants is also linked to family and lifestyle reasons, rather than just the income opportunities in different countries (Gibson and McKenzie 2011). About 30 percent of the migrants in the EU return to their home countries within a decade. This share increases to more than 40 percent among high-skilled migrants from the EU15, but return rates among high-skilled migrants from the NMS13 are significantly lower (figure 5.11).[5] The large gaps in wages, social services, and other amenities that fuel emigration in the first place also hinder the capacity of lagging regions to incentivize the return migration of the highly skilled. Lagging regions are thus not able to reap an important part of the benefits of emigration when high-skilled emigration turns permanent. Box 5.2 analyzes the case of recent emigration from Spain and the government's efforts to address some of the challenges for promoting return migration of the high-skilled diaspora. Chapter 7 provides a more detailed analysis of policies to enhance the mobility of skilled workers across regions and countries, defined hereby as "brain circulation" (a term the authors prefer to the negatively connoted "brain drain"), and to facilitate the return of skilled migrants.

FIGURE 5.11

Share of emigrants who return, by educational attainment, by region of origin

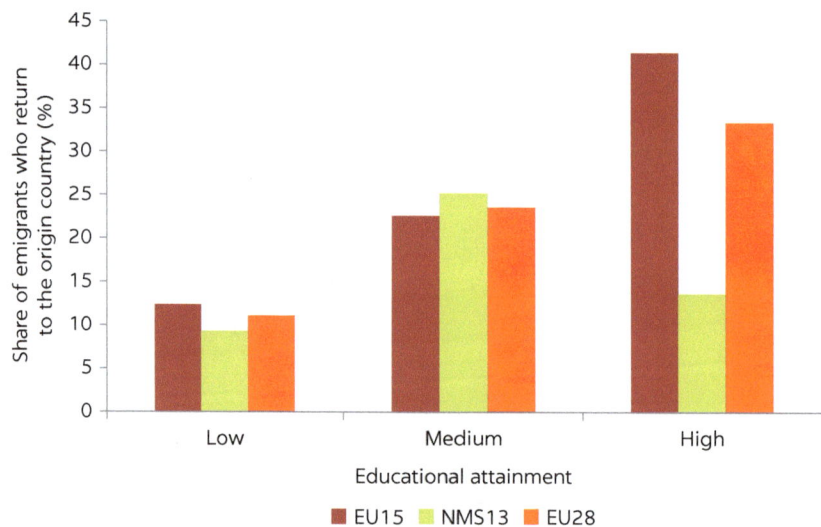

Sources: Estimates based on data from the CEPII GeoDist Database, Centre d'Etudes Prospectives et d'Informations Internationales, Paris, http://www.cepii.fr/CEPII/en/bdd_modele/presentation .asp?id=6; DIOC (Database on Immigrants in OECD and Non-OECD Countries), reference years 2010/11, Organisation for Economic Co-operation and Development, Paris, https://www.oecd.org/els /mig/dioc.htm; "2014 Labour Market Situation of Migrants and Their Immediate Descendants," LFS Ad Hoc Module, EU-LFS (European Union Labour Force Survey) (database), Eurostat, European Commission, Luxembourg, https://ec.europa.eu/eurostat/statistics-explained/index.php?title=EU _labour_force_survey_%E2%80%93_data_and_publication.
Note: Low educational attainment refers to those with less than upper secondary education, medium educational attainment refers to those with upper secondary education, and high educational attainment refers to individuals with tertiary education. Returnee rates are estimated by dividing the number of returnees in 2014 by the stock of migrants in 2010 and multiplying by the elasticity of returnees to migrants, (the percentage change in returnees for a 1 percent change in the number of migrants) which is derived from a gravity-type equation that controls for a set of geographical and social ties between the sending and receiving countries, including distance, contiguity, share of common ethnic groups. EU15 = European Union members before 2004 (Austria, Belgium, Denmark, Finland, France, Germany, Greece, Ireland, Italy, Luxembourg, the Netherlands, Portugal, Spain, Sweden, and the United Kingdom); EU28 = EU15 + NMS13; NMS13 = New Member States joining in 2004, 2007, and 2013 (Bulgaria, Croatia, Cyprus, the Czech Republic, Estonia, Hungary, Latvia, Lithuania, Malta, Poland, Romania, the Slovak Republic, and Slovenia).

Box 5.2

Emigration from Spain and the government's efforts to attract the young diaspora

Over the last decades Spain has been a paradigmatic case among European Union (EU) countries with large swings of migration flows. Contrary to the experience of other countries in the region, Spain was a net emigrant country until the 1970s, and it was not until the end of the 1990s that immigration flows rapidly accelerated. The immigration boom was unprecedented in terms of size and speed. In just over a decade, the stock of foreign-born population increased from 1 million to 6.7 million (figure B5.2.1, panel a). At the peak, migrants represented 14.3 percent of the total population, making Spain one of the largest immigrant-receiving countries in the EU. By contrast, migration outflows were negligible until the end of the 2000s.

The effects of the Great Recession on the Spanish labor market were very pronounced and reduced the attractiveness of Spain as a migrant-receiving country. After 2008, employment fell by almost 18.5 percent and the unemployment rate peaked at 26.9 percent at the beginning of 2013. Particularly worrisome was the

deterioration of youth unemployment, which reached over 55 percent, and was 40 percent among the immigrant population. As a result, Spain rapidly transitioned from large immigration to vast emigration. At the peak of the recession in 2013, 460,000 foreigners left Spain, moving the migration balance of population without Spanish nationality to a net outflow of 210,000 (figure B5.2.1, panel b).

The migration outflows were composed not only of migrants returning to their home countries but also of an increasing number of Spaniards who decided to move abroad. In the last decade, the diaspora of Spanish nationals has increased by 1 million, reaching more than 2.5 million in 2019 (figure B5.2.1, panel a). A big part of those outflows consisted of foreign-born individuals who became naturalized and then decided to return to their home countries. Still, about 830,000 people born in Spain are currently residing abroad. Recent emigrants from Spain are younger and more highly educated than Spaniards who stay in Spain. About 70 percent are less than 35 years old, mostly

FIGURE B5.2.1

Stock and flows of immigration and emigration in Spain

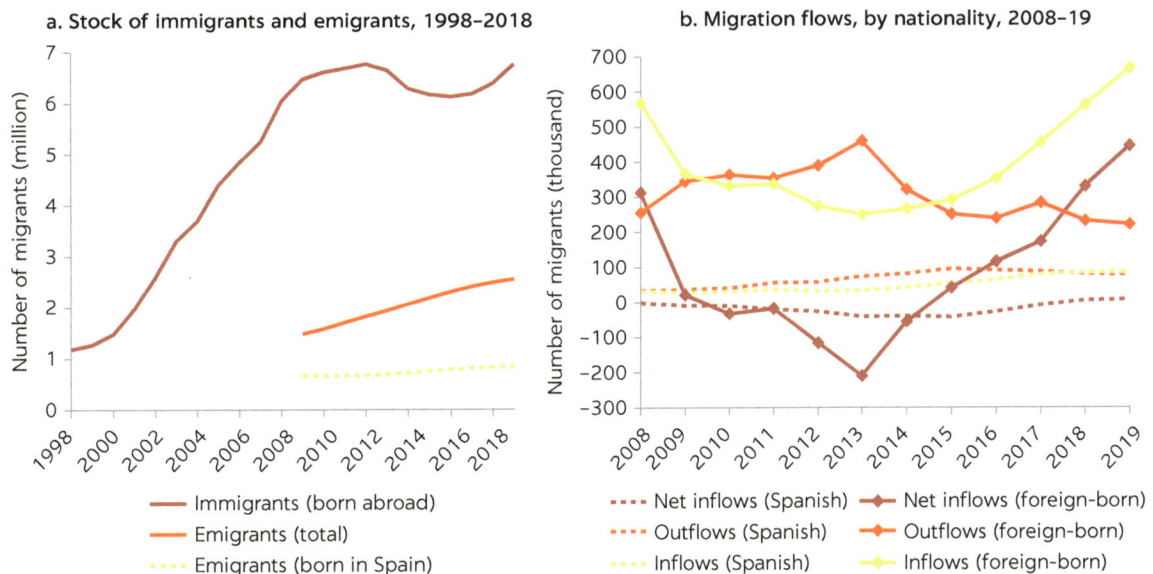

a. Stock of immigrants and emigrants, 1998–2018

b. Migration flows, by nationality, 2008–19

Source: Instituto Nacional de Estadista (Spanish Statistical Office).
Note: Net inflows are defined as inflows minus outflows of the corresponding population.

continued

Box 5.2, *continued*

migrating to other EU countries (51 percent), Latin America (26 percent), or the United States (7 percent). As Izquierdo, Jimeno, and Lacuesta (2016) show, almost half of Spanish emigrants have a tertiary education, compared to 32 percent of the nonemigrant population.

Since 2017, Spain has returned to net migration inflows, and the number of immigrants has increased again to precrisis levels (figure B5.2.1, panel a). At the same time, although emigration flows of nationals have decreased, there is a persistent challenge to attract the young educated diaspora back, which has become one of the government's priorities. According to a survey of 765 current young emigrants, INJUVE (2014) finds that about four in five emigrants have the desire to return to Spain, although most do not have concrete plans to do so.

Recent government policies have been implemented in order to strengthen the links with the Spanish diaspora and promote brain circulation and the return of young Spaniards. The Secretary General of Immigration and Emigration provides information online about job opportunities abroad for the young unemployed and engages with Spanish consulates to help integrate Spanish emigrants (Arango 2016). In 2019, it published the "Plan de retorno a España," made up of 50 measures to remove personal, professional, and administrative barriers to return to Spain, including assistance to plan the return and define a professional plan (SGIE 2019). Furthermore, the Spanish State Employment Service elaborated a plan to address the problem of high youth unemployment; one of the plan's measures is to create a program to incentivize the return of the young diaspora and support mobility (SEPE 2019). It includes support for self-employment and finding employment, and financial help for moving back to Spain and finding lodging. It also provides assistance for returnees with one-stop shops that include information about available resources at different public administrations and their procedures, employment offers, and networks of returnees. One key element is the active participation of interested firms in the process, to connect labor supply and demand. Although the actual return of young emigrants is largely linked to employment opportunities in Spain, these measures can smooth the transition and reduce bureaucratic and information barriers while keeping stronger links with the diaspora.

When able to convince emigrants to return, sending countries and regions can benefit from the associated knowledge transfers and spillovers that increase productivity. When migrants return to their home countries, they bring back productive skills, new work experiences, different social norms, links with international networks, and knowledge of technological change that can be valuable in domestic labor markets (Clemens, Özden, and Rapoport 2014; Le 2008; Rapoport 2004). Returnees often become entrepreneurs who can have positive effects on employment among workers who stayed (Hausmann and Nedelkoska 2017; Kilic et al. 2009; Piracha and Vadean 2010). Thus, in the long run, brain circulation may result in brain gain rather than a drain of human resources, benefiting both sending and receiving countries (Boeri et al. 2012; Mayr and Peri 2008).

Return migration varies by educational attainment, country of origin, and country of destination. Among emigrants from the EU15, higher educational attainment is associated with a greater expected propensity to return, that is, 41 percent among highly skilled workers relative to 12 percent among low-skilled workers (see figure 5.11). The positive correlation between educational attainment and the estimated returnee rate is less evident in the NMS13. There, the greatest propensity to return occurs among workers with midlevel skills, whereas highly skilled workers are significantly less likely to return (14 percent). Overall, the prevalence of returnees among emigrants from the EU15 and emigrants from the NMS13 is similar across low and midlevel educational attainment, but there is a large divergence across more highly skilled migrants. These individuals are three times more likely to return to their countries of origin if they are from the EU15 than if they are from the NMS13.

Migrants from the NMS13 who emigrated to non-EU Organisation for Economic Co-operation and Development countries show an even lower propensity to return than those who emigrated to the EU15. NMS13 emigrants returning from non-European countries—particularly developed economies such as Australia, Canada, and the United States—show a substantially lower likelihood of returning relative to NMS13 emigrants to the EU15 (figure 5.12). The return rates among EU15 emigrants are similar across subregions of destination, although, overall, they are slightly higher among EU15 returnees from non-European countries relative to EU15 returnees from other EU15 countries.

FIGURE 5.12

Return rates of migrants from the EU28, by educational attainment and migration corridor

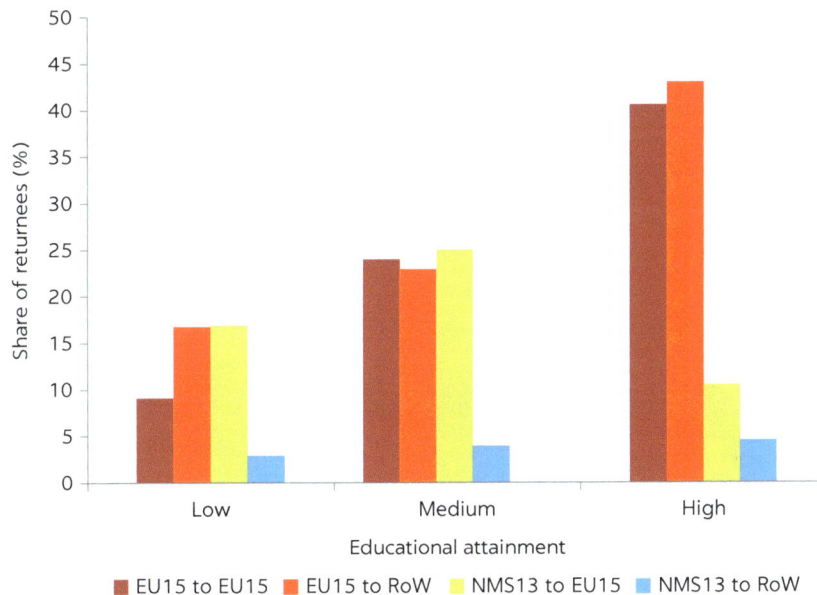

Sources: Estimates based on data from the CEPII GeoDist Database, Centre d'Etudes Prospectives et d'Informations Internationales, Paris, http://www.cepii.fr/CEPII/en/bdd_modele/presentation .asp?id=6; DIOC (Database on Immigrants in OECD and Non-OECD Countries), reference years 2010/11, Organisation for Economic Co-operation and Development, Paris, https://www.oecd.org/els /mig/dioc.htm; "2014 Labour Market Situation of Migrants and Their Immediate Descendants," LFS Ad Hoc Module, EU-LFS (European Union Labour Force Survey) (database), Eurostat, European Commission, Luxembourg, https://ec.europa.eu/eurostat/statistics-explained/index.php/EU_labour _force_survey.
Note: Low educational attainment refers to those with less than upper secondary education, medium educational attainment refers to those with upper secondary education, and high educational attainment refers to individuals with tertiary education. EU15 = European Union members before 2004 (Austria, Belgium, Denmark, Finland, France, Germany, Greece, Ireland, Italy, Luxembourg, the Netherlands, Portugal, Spain, Sweden, and the United Kingdom); NMS13 = New Member States joining in 2004, 2007, and 2013 (Bulgaria, Croatia, Cyprus, the Czech Republic, Estonia, Hungary, Latvia, Lithuania, Malta, Poland, Romania, the Slovak Republic, and Slovenia); RoW = rest of the world.

Furthermore, skilled migrants from the NMS13 show a lower propensity to return compared to skilled migrants from the EU15.

Returnees in the NMS13 are more likely to become self-employed and therefore to start up new activities; they also earn higher wages if they work as salaried employees. The literature on the integration of returning migrants in home labor markets in developing countries suggests that the migration experience increases the wages of return migrants back home (Reinhold and Thom 2013; Wahba 2015). In Eastern Europe, the results indicate substantive wage premiums among returnees compared to nonmigrants, ranging from 40 percent in Hungary and from 10 percent to 45 percent in a selected group of countries, including Romania, to almost 100 percent in Albania (Ambrosini et al. 2015; Co, Gang, and Yun 2000; de Coulon and Piracha 2005; Martin and Radu 2012). Most recent data on the NMS13 also show positive premiums for return migrants in almost all countries (figure 5.13, panel a). Returnees are between 10 and 30 percentage points more likely than nonmigrants to be in the top three deciles of earnings, except in the Czech Republic and Slovenia. The largest earnings premiums among returnees are observed in Bulgaria, Estonia, Latvia, and the Slovak Republic. Returnees are also more likely than nonmigrants to be self-employed in several countries, including Bulgaria, Romania, and the Slovak Republic (figure 5.13, panel b). These results are in line with past studies and highlight the role of returnees in promoting self-employment and entrepreneurship, thanks to savings accumulated abroad, which have the potential to create new jobs and revitalize local economies.[6]

FIGURE 5.13

Gaps in labor market outcomes, returnees relative to nonmigrants, NMS13

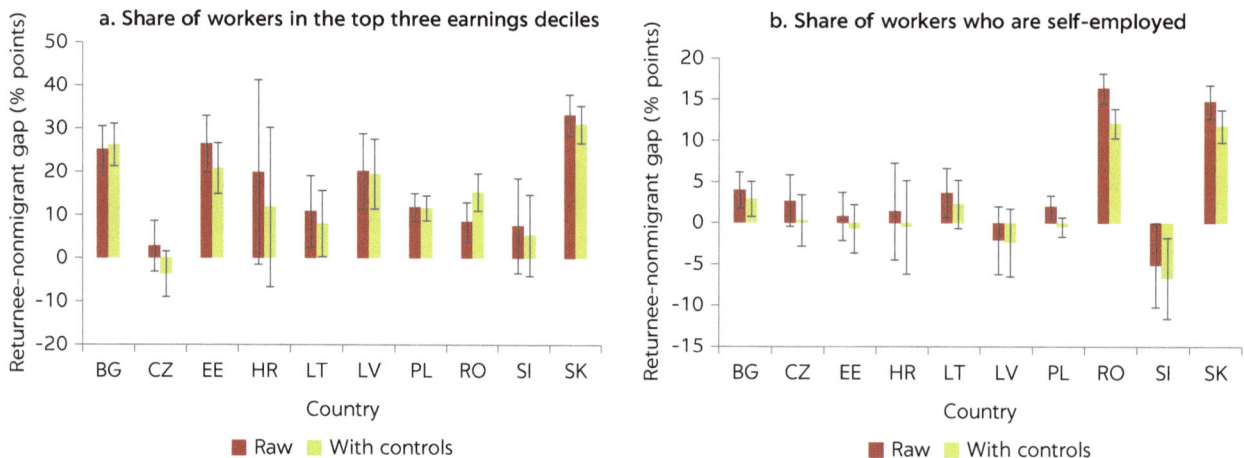

Source: Estimates drawn from data in "2014 Labour Market Situation of Migrants and Their Immediate Descendants," LFS Ad Hoc Module, European Union Labour Force Survey (database), Eurostat, European Commission, Luxembourg, https://ec.europa.eu/eurostat/statistics-explained/index.php/EU_labour _force_survey.

Note: Raw (unconditional) gaps are based on differences in the means of returnees relative to stayers (with no controls). The gaps with controls are the betas of regressions of returnees on a dummy for being in the top three earnings deciles or for being self-employed, controlling for age, gender, education, and region of resettlement. For comparison, figure includes 95 percent confidence intervals. NMS13 = New Member States joining the European Union in 2004, 2007, and 2013 (Bulgaria, Croatia, Cyprus, the Czech Republic, Estonia, Hungary, Latvia, Lithuania, Malta, Poland, Romania, the Slovak Republic, and Slovenia).

NOTES

1. The EU15's full membership before 2004 consisted of Austria, Belgium, Denmark, Finland, France, Germany, Greece, Ireland, Italy, Luxembourg, the Netherlands, Portugal, Spain, Sweden, and the United Kingdom.
2. The NMS13 (with year of accession) consists of the following: Cyprus, the Czech Republic, Estonia, Hungary, Latvia, Lithuania, Malta, Poland, the Slovak Republic, and Slovenia (2004); Bulgaria and Romania (2007); and Croatia (2013).
3. The European Commission provides statistics on the migration of doctors and other regulated professions; see the Regulated Professions Database, European Commission, Brussels, https://ec.europa.eu/growth/tools-databases/regprof/index.cfm?action=homepage. The EU15 north is Austria, Belgium, Denmark, Finland, France, Germany, Ireland, Luxembourg, the Netherlands, Sweden, and the United Kingdom. The EU15 south is Greece, Italy, Portugal, and Spain.
4. The NMS10 consists of Cyprus, the Czech Republic, Estonia, Hungary, Latvia, Lithuania, Malta, Poland, the Slovak Republic, and Slovenia.
5. These estimates are based on the number of emigrants from the total diaspora in 2010 who had returned to their countries of origin by 2014.
6. For prior evidence on the higher propensity of return migrants to start self-employment activities outside the EU, see McCormick and Wahba (2001), Dustmann and Kirchkamp (2002), Mesnard (2004), Kilic et al. (2009), Piracha and Vadean (2010), Wahba and Zenou (2012), and Bossavie et al. (2021).

REFERENCES

Abarcar, Paolo, and Caroline Theoharides. 2018. "The International Migration of Healthcare Professionals and the Supply of Educated Individuals Left Behind." Paper presented at the panel on "Migration and Employment Mobility," Association for Public Policy Analysis and Management's fall research conference, "Evidence for Action: Encouraging Innovation and Improvement," Washington, DC, November 8–10.

Adams, Richard H., and John Page. 2005. "Do International Migration and Remittances Reduce Poverty in Developing Countries?" *World Development* 33 (10): 1645–69.

Agrawal, Ajay K., Devesh Kapur, John McHale, and Alexander Oettl. 2011. "Brain Drain or Brain Bank? The Impact of Skilled Emigration on Poor-Country Innovation." NBER Working Paper 14592 (December), National Bureau of Economic Research, Cambridge, MA.

Ambrosini, J. William, Karin Mayr, Giovanni Peri, and Dragos Radu. 2015. "The Selection of Migrants and Returnees in Romania: Evidence and Long-Run Implications." *Economics of Transition and Institutional Change* 23 (4): 753–93.

Amuedo-Dorantes, Catalina, and Susan Pozo. 2010. "Accounting for Remittance and Migration Effects on Children's Schooling." *World Development* 38 (12): 1747–59.

Anelli, Massimo, Gaetano Basso, Giuseppe Ippedico, and Giovanni Peri. 2019. "Youth Drain, Entrepreneurship, and Innovation." NBER Working Paper 26055 (July), National Bureau of Economic Research, Cambridge, MA.

Arango, Joaquin. 2016. "Emigration: New Emigration Policies Needed for an Emerging Diaspora." Migration Policy Institute, Washington, DC.

Atoyan, Ruben, Lone Christiansen, Allan Dizioli, Christian Ebeke, Nadeem Ilahi, Anna Ilyina, Gil Mehrez, et al. 2016. "Emigration and Its Economic Impact on Eastern Europe." IMF Staff Discussion Note SDN/16/07 (July), International Monetary Fund, Washington, DC.

Bahar, Dany, and Hillel Rapoport. 2018. "Migration, Knowledge Diffusion, and the Comparative Advantage of Nations." *Economic Journal* 128 (612): F273–F305.

Barsbai, Toman, Hillel Rapoport, Andreas Steinmayr, and Christoph Trebesch, 2017. "The Effect of Labor Migration on the Diffusion of Democracy: Evidence from a Former Soviet Republic." *American Economic Journal: Applied Economics* 9 (3): 36–69.

Beine, Michel, Cecily Defoort, and Frédéric Docquier. 2011. "A Panel Data Analysis of the Brain Gain." *World Development* 39 (4): 523–32.

Beine, Michel, Frédéric Docquier, and Hillel Rapoport. 2001. "Brain Drain and Economic Growth: Theory and Evidence." *Journal of Development Economics* 64 (1): 275–89.

Beine, Michel, Frédéric Docquier, and Hillel Rapoport. 2008. "Brain Drain and Human Capital Formation in Developing Countries: Winners and Losers." *Economic Journal* 118 (528): 631–52.

Bijward, Govert, Christian Schluter, and Jackline Wahba. 2014. "The Impact of Labour Market Dynamics on the Return Decision of Immigrants." *The Review of Economics and Statistics* 96 (3): 483–94.

Boeri, Tito, Herbert Brücker, Frederic Docquier, and Hillel Rapoport. 2012. *Brain Drain and Brain Gain: The Global Competition to Attract High-skilled Migrants*. Oxford: Oxford University Press.

Bossavie, Laurent, Joseph-Simon Goerlach, Caglar Ozden, and He Wang. 2021. "Temporary Migration for Long-term Investment." Policy Research Working Paper Series 9740, World Bank, Washington, DC.

Chami, Ralph, Dalia Hakura, and Peter Montiel. 2009. "Remittances: An Automatic Output Stabilizer?" IMF Working Paper 09/91, International Monetary Fund, Washington, DC.

Clemens, Michael A., Çağlar Özden, and Hillel Rapoport. 2014. "Migration and Development Research Is Moving Far beyond Remittances." *World Development* 64 (December): 121–24.

Clements, Benedict J., Kamil Dybczak, Vitor Gaspar, Sanjeev Gupta, and Mauricio Soto. 2015. "The Fiscal Consequences of Shrinking Populations." IMF Staff Discussion Note SDN 15/21 (October 26), International Monetary Fund, Washington, DC.

Co, Catherine Y., Ira N. Gang, and Myeong-Su Yun. 2000. "Returns to Returning." *Journal of Population Economics* 13 (1): 57–79.

de Coulon, Augustin, and Matloob Piracha. 2005. "Self-Selection and the Performance of Return Migrants: The Source Country Perspective." *Journal of Population Economics* 18 (4): 779–807.

Desai, Mihir A., Devesh Kapur, John McHale, and Keith Rogers. 2009. "The Fiscal Impact of High-Skilled Emigration: Flows of Indians to the U.S." *Journal of Development Economics* 88 (1): 32–44.

Docquier, Frédéric, and Elisabetta Lodigiani. 2010. "Skilled Migration and Business Networks." *Open Economies Review* 21 (4): 565–88.

Docquier, Frédéric, Elisabetta Lodigiani, Hillel Rapoport, and Maurice Schiff. 2011. "Emigration and Democracy." Policy Research Working Paper 5557, World Bank, Washington, DC.

Docquier, Frédéric, Çağlar Özden, and Giovanni Peri. 2014. "The Labour Market Effects of Immigration and Emigration in OECD Countries." *VoxEU*, October 6. https://voxeu.org/article/labour-market-effects-migration-oecd-countries.

Docquier, Frédéric, and Hillel Rapoport. 2009. "Documenting the Brain Drain of 'La Crème de la Crème': Three Case-Studies on International Migration at the Upper Tail of the Education Distribution." *Journal of Economics and Statistics* 229 (6): 679–705.

Docquier, Frederic, and Hillel Rapoport. 2012. "Globalization, Brain Drain and Development." *Journal of Economic Literature* 50 (3): 681–730.

Docquier, Frédéric, Riccardo Turati, Jérôme Valette, and Chrysovalantis Vasilakis. 2018. "Birthplace Diversity and Economic Growth: Evidence from the US States in the Post–World War II Period." IZA Discussion Paper 11802, Institute of Labor Economics, Bonn.

Dustmann, Christian, Tommaso Frattini, and Anna Cecilia Rosso. 2015. "The Effect of Emigration from Poland on Polish Wages." *Scandinavian Journal of Economics* 117 (2): 522–64.

Dustmann, Christian, and Joseph-Simon Goerlach. 2016. "The Economics of Temporary Migrations." *Journal of Economic Literature* 54 (1): 98–136.

Dustmann, Christian, and Oliver Kirchkamp. 2002. "The Optimal Migration Duration and Activity Choice after Re-migration." *Journal of Development Economics* 67 (2): 351–72.

Dustmann, Christian, and Yoram Weiss. 2007. "Return Migration: Theory and Empirical Evidence from the UK." *British Journal of Industrial Relations* 45 (2): 236–56.

Elsner, Benjamin. 2013. "Emigration and Wages: The EU Enlargement Experiment." *Journal of International Economics* 91 (1): 154–63.

Farchy, Emily. 2009. "The Impact of EU Accession on Human Capital Formation: Can Migration Fuel a Brain Gain?" Policy Research Working Paper 4845. World Bank, Washington, DC.

Genc, Murat, Masood Gheasi, Jacques Poot, and Peter Nijkamp. 2012. "The Impact of Immigration on International Trade: A Meta-Analysis." In *Migration Impact Assessment: New Horizons*, edited by Peter Nijkamp, Jacques Poot, and Mediha Sahin, 301–37. New Horizons in Regional Science Series. Cheltenham, UK: Edward Elgar.

Gibson, John, and David McKenzie. 2011. "The Microeconomic Determinants of Emigration and Return Migration of the Best and Brightest: Evidence from the Pacific." *Journal of Development Economics* 95 (1): 18–29.

Gibson, John, and David McKenzie. 2012. "The Economic Consequences of 'Brain Drain' of the Best and Brightest: Microeconomic Evidence from Five Countries." *Economic Journal* 122 (560): 339–75.

Giesing, Yvonne, and Nadzeya Laurentsyeva. 2017. "Firms Left Behind: Emigration and Firm Productivity." CESifo Working Paper 6815 (December), Munich Society for the Promotion of Economic Research, Center for Economic Studies, Ludwig Maximilian University and Ifo Institute for Economic Research, Munich.

Gould, David M. 1994. "Immigrant Links to the Home Countries: Empirical Implications for U.S. Bilateral Trade Flows." *Review of Economics and Statistics* 76 (2): 302–16.

Greif, Avner. 1993. "Contract Enforceability and Economic Institutions in Early Trade: The Maghribi Traders' Coalition." *American Economic Review* 83 (3): 525–48.

Hausmann, Ricardo, and Ljubica Nedelkoska. 2018. "Welcome Home in a Crisis: Effects of Return Migration on the Non-migrants' Wages and Employment." *European Economic Review* 101 (January): 101–32.

Head, Keith, and John Reis. 1998. "Immigration and Trade Creation: Econometric Evidence from Canada." *Canadian Journal of Economics* 31 (1): 47–62.

Herander, Mark G., and Luz A. Saavedra. 2005. "Exports and the Structure of Immigrant-based Networks: The Role of Geographic Proximity." *Review of Economics and Statistics* 87 (2): 323–35.

Hildebrandt, Nicole, and David J. McKenzie. 2005. "The Effects of Migration on Child Health in Mexico." *Economia* 6 (1): 257–89.

INJUVE (Instituto de la Juventud). 2014. "La emigración de los jóvenes españoles en el contexto de la crisis: Análisis y datos de un fenómeno difícil de cuantificar." Observatorio de la Juventud en España, Madrid. http://www.injuve.es/sites/default/files /adjuntos/2019/05/emigracion_jovenes_2014.pdf.

Izquierdo, Mario, Juan F. Jimeno and Aitor Lacuesta. 2016. "Spain: From Immigration to Emigration?" *IZA Journal of Migration* 5, article 10. https://izajodm.springeropen.com /articles/10.1186/s40176-016-0058-y.

Kerr, William R. 2008. "Ethnic Scientific Communities and International Technology Diffusion." *Review of Economics and Statistics* 90 (3): 518–37.

Kilic, Talip, Calogero Carletto, Benjamin Davis, and Alberto Zezza. 2009. "Investing Back Home: Return Migration and Business Ownership in Albania." *Economics of Transition and Institutional Change* 17 (3): 587–623.

Kugler, Maurice, and Hillel Rapoport. 2007. "International Labor and Capital Flows: Complements or Substitutes?" *Economics Letters* 94 (2): 155–62.

Le, Thanh. 2008. "'Brain Drain' or 'Brain Circulation': Evidence from OECD's International Migration and R&D Spillovers." *Scottish Journal of Political Economy* 55 (5): 618–36.

Martin, Reiner, and Dragos Radu. 2012. "Return Migration: The Experience of Eastern Europe." *Journal of International Migration* 50 (6): 109–28.

Mayr, Karin, and Giovanni Peri. 2008. "Return Migration as a Channel of Brain Gain." NBER Working Paper 14039 (May), National Bureau of Economic Research, Cambridge, MA.

Mayr, Karin, and Giovanni Peri. 2009. "Brain Drain and Brain Return: Theory and Application to Eastern-Western Europe." *B. E. Journal of Economic Analysis and Policy* 9 (1): 1–52.

McCormick, Barry, and Jackline Wahba. 2001. "Overseas Work Experience, Savings and Entrepreneurship Amongst Return Migrants to LDCs." *Scottish Journal of Political Economy* 48(2): 164–78.

Mendola, Mariapia, and Calogero Carletto. 2012. "Migration and Gender Differences in the Home Labour Market: Evidence from Albania." *Labour Economics* 19 (6): 870–80.

Mesnard, Alice. 2004. "Temporary Migration and Capital Market Imperfection." *Oxford Economic Papers* 56(2): 242–62.

Orefice, Gianluca, Hillel Rapoport, and Gianluca Santoni. 2021. "How Do Immigrants Promote Exports?," Working Papers DT/2021/04, DIAL (Développement, Institutions et Mondialisation), Paris.

Pandey, Abhishek, Alok Aggarwal, Richard Devane, and Yevgeny Kuznetsov. 2006. "The Indian Diaspora: A Unique Case?" In *Diaspora Networks and the International Migration of Skills: How Countries Can Draw on Their Talent Abroad,* edited by Yevgeny Kuznetsov, 71–98. WDI Development Studies Series. Washington, DC: World Bank.

Peri, Giovanni, and Francisco Requena-Silvente. 2010. "The Trade Creation Effect of Immigrants: Evidence from the Remarkable Case of Spain." *Canadian Journal of Economics* 43 (4): 1433–59.

Piracha, Matloob, and Florin Petru Vadean. 2010. "Return Migration and Occupational Choice: Evidence from Albania." *World Development* 38 (8): 1141–55.

Rapoport, Hillel. 2004. "Who Is Afraid of the Brain Drain? Human Capital Flight and Growth in Developing Countries." *Brussels Economic Review* 47 (1): 89–101.

Rauch, James E., and Alessandra Casella. 2003. "Overcoming Informational Barriers to International Resource Allocation: Prices and Ties." *Economic Journal* 113 (484): 21–42.

Rauch, James E., and Vitor Trindade. 2002. "Ethnic Chinese Networks in International Trade." *Review of Economics and Statistics* 84 (1): 116–30.

Roman, Monica, and Zizi Goschin. 2014. "Return Migration in an Economic Crisis Context. A Survey on Romanian Healthcare Professionals." *Romanian Journal of Economics* 39 (2): 100–20.

Reinhold, Steffen, and Kevin Thom. 2013. "Migration Experience and Earnings in the Mexican Labor Market." *Journal of Human Resources* 48 (3): 768–820.

Saxenian AnnaLee. 2002. "Local and Global Networks of Immigrant Professional in Silicon Valley." Public Policy Institute of California, San Francisco.

SEPE (Spanish State Employment Service). 2019. "Plan de Choque por el Empleo Joven 2019–2021." Ministerio de Trabajo, Migraciones y Seguridad Social. https://www.sepe.es/HomeSepe/Personas/encontrar-trabajo/plan-de-choque-empleo-2019-2021.

SGIE (Secretary General of Immigration and Emigration). 2019. "Plan de Retorno a España." SGIE, Madrid. https://www.boe.es/boe/dias/2019/03/30/pdfs/BOE-A-2019-4705.pdf.

Spilimbergo, Antonio. 2009. "Democracy and Foreign Education." *American Economic Review* 99 (1): 528–43.

Wahba, Jackline. 2015. "Selection, Selection, Selection: The Impact of Return Migration." *Journal of Population Economics* 28 (3): 535–63.

Wahba, Jackline, and Yves Zenou. 2012. "Out of Sight, Out of Mind: Migration, Entrepreneurship and Social Capital" *Regional Science and Urban Economics* 42(5): 890–903.

Wescott, Clay Goodloe, and Jennifer M. Brinkerhoff. 2006. *Converting Migration Drains into Gains: Harnessing the Resources of Overseas Professionals.* September. Manila: Asian Development Bank.

6 The Implications of COVID-19 for Migrants in the European Union

COVID-19 (coronavirus) has restricted labor mobility and exerted pressure on the European Union (EU) labor market. On the supply side, the COVID-19 crisis has created unequal disruptions across occupations. To prevent contagion, governments have restricted mobility for work to sectors that are considered essential to the economy. Jobs that are not considered essential or amenable to being carried out remotely—that is, at home—are therefore the most highly exposed to supply constraints. On the demand side, some sectors suffer from more severe falloffs in demand in the short and medium terms, such as airlines and all activities related to tourism, whereas other sectors may experience greater demand, for example, health care. On top of the risks of job losses, workers vary in their exposure and health risks related to COVID-19. Thus, essential activities that cannot be carried out from home and, at the same time, require extensive face-to-face interactions, such as health care, are especially exposed to health risks

For any given level of education, migrants are more vulnerable to supply and demand shocks and are more exposed to COVID-19 health risks. Analysis of occupations shows that migrants are more highly exposed to the risk of supply disruptions, particularly because they are typically less likely to perform telework and are more likely to have essential jobs that entail more interactions with others and thus greater exposure to COVID-19 contagion (figure 6.1, panels a and b). This means they have less access to safe jobs, that is, jobs that can be performed from home or jobs that, although considered essential, involve less face-to-face interaction with clients or providers and are therefore associated with less risk of contagion (figure 6.1, panel c). Based on the potential demand reduction in the coming months, migrants are also likely to face greater demand shock (figure 6.1, panel d).[1]

Migrants from the NMS13 (the 13 New Member States joining the EU in 2004, 2007, and 2013) are more highly exposed to COVID-19 relative to migrants from the EU15.[2] Migrants from the NMS13 are 4 percentage points more likely than the average migrant in the EU and 6 percentage points more likely than natives to have jobs that are not essential and not amenable to telework. The native-born population and migrants from the EU15 show similar vulnerabilities and exposure to COVID-19 in the labor market. Migrants from the NMS13 and migrants from developing countries outside the EU28 are 8 percentage points more likely than natives to have jobs associated with greater health risks (23 percent and 15 percent, respectively), whereas natives and migrants from the EU15 exhibit similar occupational choices and risks.[3]

COVID-19 affects low-skilled migrants more severely than those with higher educational levels, which has important implications on the profile of return migrants. As figure 6.1 shows, supply restrictions, demand declines, and exposure to health risks are unequally distributed across workers. The probability of being employed in better-protected jobs that can be performed from home or that require little face-to-face interaction is significantly greater among workers with more advanced educational attainment, whereas individuals with lower levels of education have jobs that are associated with higher risks of disruption. Increases in unemployment arising because of the COVID-19 crisis may thus affect

FIGURE 6.1

Job vulnerability in the EU, by place of birth and educational attainment

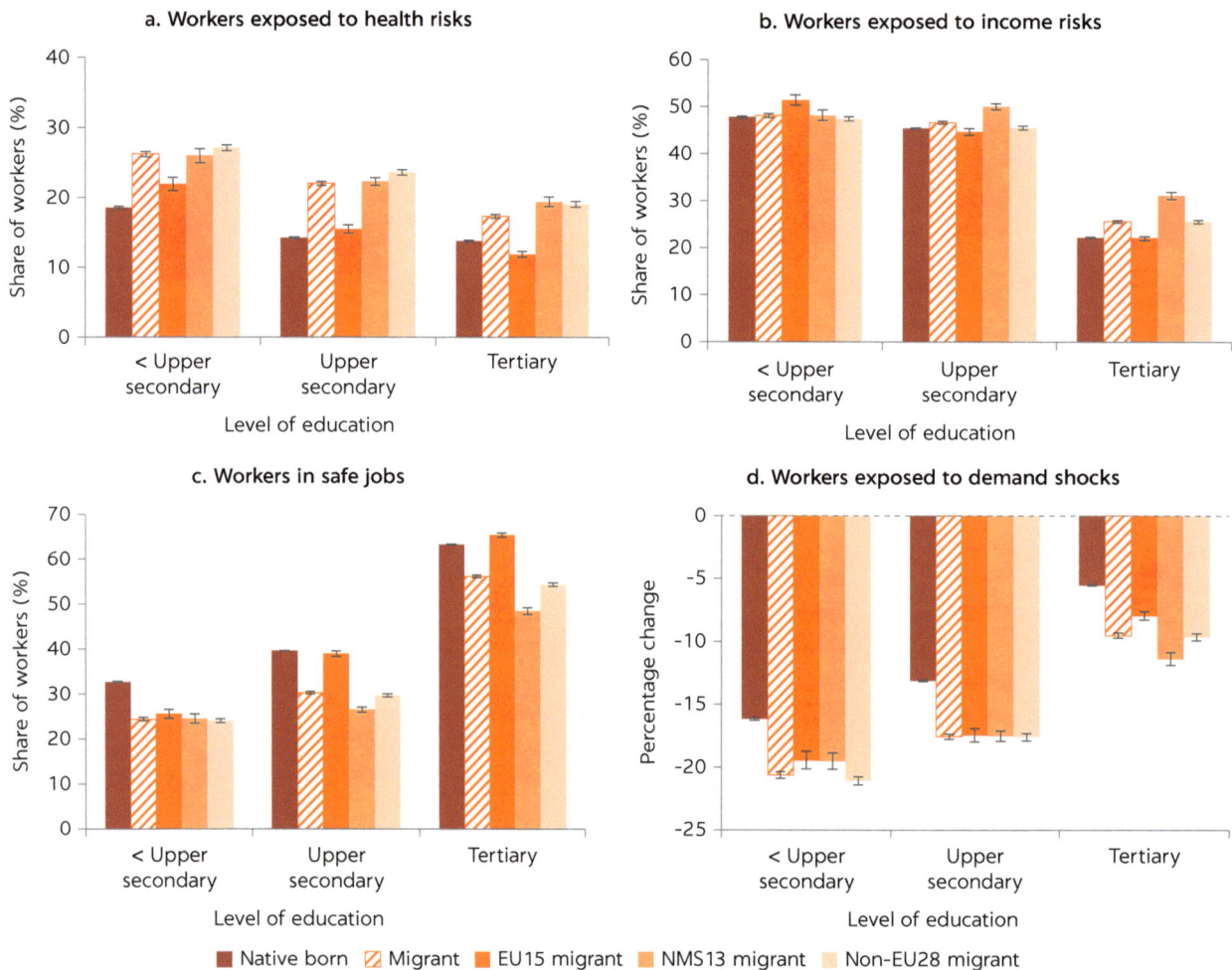

Legend: ■ Native born ▨ Migrant ■ EU15 migrant ■ NMS13 migrant ■ Non-EU28 migrant

Source: Elaborations based on 2018 data from the European Union Labour Force Survey (database), Eurostat, European Commission, Luxembourg, https://ec.europa.eu/eurostat/statistics-explained/index.php/EU_labour_force_survey and estimates of Avdiu and Nayyar 2020; CBO 2006; del Río–Chanona et al. 2020; Dingel and Neiman 2020; Fasani and Mazza 2020; Pfeiffer, Roeger, and in 't Veld 2020.
Note: Occupations exposed to health risks are those that are considered essential by governments, have not been interrupted during lockdowns, cannot be performed from home, and require substantial face-to-face interactions. Occupations exposed to supply shocks are those that are not essential and cannot be done from home. Safe occupations are all those that can be done from home or are essential but require little face-to-face interaction. The expected demand shock is based on simulations of sectoral demand responses to past virus contagions.
EU15 = European Union members before 2004 (Austria, Belgium, Denmark, Finland, France, Germany, Greece, Ireland, Italy, Luxembourg, the Netherlands, Portugal, Spain, Sweden, and the United Kingdom); EU28 = EU15 + NMS13; NMS13 = New Member States joining in 2004, 2007, and 2013 (Bulgaria, Croatia, Cyprus, the Czech Republic, Estonia, Hungary, Latvia, Lithuania, Malta, Poland, Romania, the Slovak Republic, and Slovenia).

low-skilled migrants more than high-skilled migrants. Under these circumstances, various measures, such as fiscal incentives, that some governments are proposing as a response to the COVID-19 crisis to boost high-skilled migration may end up contrasting with push factors that encourage less educated migrants to return to their countries of origin.

The reduction in the stock of migrants and in employment opportunities since the COVID-19 crisis began can be expected to have important effects on remittances in the region. Different studies have shown that remittances tend to be countercyclical and to cushion economic downturns in sending countries (Frankel 2011). However, the COVID-19 crisis has hit sending and receiving countries similarly, which results in theoretically ambiguous effects on remittances. Although migrants tend to increase remittances when the needs of relatives and friends in the country of origin are higher (Gupta 2005), remittances are also shaped by factors in the host countries, particularly the size of the migrant population and their earnings (Clemens and McKenzie 2018). In line with the higher COVID-19–related occupational risks that migrants face, recent Eurostat data show a larger drop in employment among migrants between the second quarter of 2020 and the last quarter of 2019 (–5.6 percent) than among domestic-born workers (–2.3 percent). Furthermore, the deterioration of the labor market in receiving countries coupled with mobility restrictions has rapidly reduced the stock of migrants in the region. According to *International Migration Outlook 2020,* issuances of new visas and work permits in Organisation for Economic Co-operation and Development countries fell by as much as 46 percent in the first half of 2020 compared with the same period in 2019 (OECD 2020). These factors are behind the large expected reductions in remittances, which could fall by more than 15 percent in 2020 in the region of Europe and Central Asia (World Bank 2020), the largest recorded drop in recent history.

NOTES

1. For a more detailed analysis of migrant workers' vulnerability to COVID-19, see Bossavie et al. (2020).
2. The NMS13 (with year of accession) consists of the following: Cyprus, the Czech Republic, Estonia, Hungary, Latvia, Lithuania, Malta, Poland, the Slovak Republic, and Slovenia (2004); Bulgaria and Romania (2007); and Croatia (2013). The EU15's full membership before 2004 consisted of Austria, Belgium, Denmark, Finland, France, Germany, Greece, Ireland, Italy, Luxembourg, the Netherlands, Portugal, Spain, Sweden, and the United Kingdom.
3. The EU28 represents the full EU membership before the departure of the United Kingdom in 2020 (Brexit)—that is, the EU15 plus the NMS13.

REFERENCES

Avdiu, Besart, and Gaurav Nayyar. 2020. "When Face-to-Face Interactions Become an Occupational Hazard: Jobs in the Time of COVID-19." Policy Research Working Paper 9240, World Bank, Washington, DC.

Bossavie, Laurent, Daniel Garrote Sanchez, Mattia Makovec, and Çağlar Özden. 2020. "Do Immigrants Shield the Locals? Exposure to COVID-Related Risks in the European Union." Policy Research Working Paper 9500, World Bank, Washington, DC.

CBO (Congressional Budget Office, United States). 2006. "A Potential Influenza Pandemic: An Update on Possible Macroeconomic Effects and Policy Issues." July 27, CBO, Congress of the United States, Washington, DC.

Clemens, Michael A. and David McKenzie. 2018. "Why Don't Remittances Appear to Affect Growth?" *Economic Journal* 128 (612): 179–209.

del Río–Chanona, R. María, Penny Mealy, Anton Pichler, François Lafond, and J. Doyne Farmer. 2020. "Supply and Demand Shocks in the COVID-19 Pandemic: An Industry and Occupation Perspective." *Covid Economics 6* (April 17): 65–103.

Dingel, Jonathan I., and Brent Neiman. 2020. "How Many Jobs Can Be Done at Home?" NBER Working Paper 26948 (June), National Bureau of Economic Research, Cambridge, MA.

Fasani, Francesco, and Jacopo Mazza. 2020. "Immigrant Key Workers: Their Contribution to Europe's COVID-19 Response." IZA Policy Paper 155 (April), Institute of Labor Economics, Bonn.

Frankel, Jeffrey. 2011. "Are Bilateral Remittances Countercyclical?" *Open Economies Review* 22 (1): 1–16.

Gupta, Poonam. 2005. "Macroeconomic Determinants of Remittances: Evidence from India." IMF Working Paper 05/224, International Monetary Fund, Washington DC.

OECD (Organisation for Economic Co-operation and Development). 2020. *International Migration Outlook 2020*. Paris: OECD Publishing. https://www.oecd.org/migration /international-migration-outlook-1999124x.htm.

Pfeiffer, Philipp, Werner Roeger, and Jan in 't Veld. 2020. "The COVID19-Pandemic in the EU: Macroeconomic Transmission and Economic Policy Response." European Economy Discussion Paper 127 (July), Publications Office of the European Union, Luxembourg.

World Bank. 2020. "Phase II: COVID-19 Crisis through a Migration Lens." Migration and Development Brief 33, KNOMAD–World Bank, Washington, DC.

7 Conclusions and Policy Implications

MANAGING THE MIGRATION PROCESS TO MAXIMIZE BENEFITS AND MITIGATE COSTS

Previous chapters have given evidence that the benefits and costs associated with economic migration, in particular skilled migration, vary not only between receiving and sending countries but also in the short run and the long run. In light of the results from the most recent economic literature, this report has discussed benefits and costs associated with skilled migration for both receiving and sending countries among European Union (EU) Member States (table 7.1). Although the benefits for receiving countries seem to substantially exceed the costs, in both the short run and the long run, the net effect of out-migration for sending countries is more difficult to determine a priori. In the short run, out-migration helps alleviate pressures from high unemployment, especially in certain disadvantaged regions and for some population groups (such as youth); but, at the same time, it induces human capital losses and exacerbates population aging.

Instead of focusing on preventing a drain of human resources, policies should also better manage the migration process and promote brain circulation, by taking advantage of intra-EU labor mobility and the consequent flows of networks, expertise, and trade. The EU's policy on the free movement of workers establishes the right of EU nationals to reside and work in any other EU country.[1] Given the legal provisions that protect the free movement of citizens within the EU, it is difficult to decrease out-migration and the drain on human resources without providing better wages and employment opportunities in the sending countries. In the medium/long run, skilled migration can become beneficial for sending countries ("brain gain") through return migration, which can enhance knowledge and productivity spillovers, and can contribute to job creation through business start-ups and entrepreneurship. However, return migration of the best and the brightest who left the country is not guaranteed, and sending countries should invest in ensuring conditions that can be conducive for the return of skilled migrants and their smooth reentry into the domestic labor market. Beyond encouraging return migration, sending countries can

TABLE 7.1 The impact of migration on sending and receiving countries

HORIZON	RECEIVING COUNTRIES		SENDING COUNTRIES	
	Benefits	Costs	Benefits	Costs
Short term	Partial relaxation of aging pressures Acquiring needed skills in the labor market	Potential displacement of certain groups of natives in the labor market (for example, unskilled workers), but no large effects overall	Alleviation of unemployment pressures, especially for youth Increased well-being and consumption through remittances	Acceleration in aging Reduction in human capital because of out-migration of more highly skilled Skill shortages for specific occupations Loss of taxpayers Fiscal loss if young highly educated workers emigrate Pressures on the funding of basic services
Long term	Acquiring needed skills in the labor market Migrants as net fiscal contributors	Pressures on social services	Incentivizes human capital accumulation, although sending countries bear the financial cost of educating part of the population leaving the country Return migration enhances technological transfers and knowledge spillovers and contributes to job creation for stayers	Acceleration in aging if the pool of return migrants remains small

Source: World Bank elaboration.

benefit from actively engaging with their diasporas to increase the positive spillovers of global know-how and networks (World Bank 2018).

Policies promoting return migration and curbing emigration flows tend to be complementary and mutually reinforcing. Both types of policies require tackling key challenges in social, economic, and political conditions in countries of origin that incentivize workers to emigrate in the first place. In the short run, policies aimed at stimulating the demand side of the labor market in sending areas and countries may be more effective at containing the drain on human resources at the margin. By contrast, policies designed to improve the supply and the quality of skills and human capital and to remove the structural gaps between sending and receiving regions will have an effect only in the medium to long run.

POLICY IMPLICATIONS IN THE SHORT RUN

As highlighted in previous chapters, migration flows in the EU are largely driven by disparities in economic opportunities across regions of Europe. Thus, reducing the short-term costs of labor mobility for sending countries by reducing emigration, or increasing its benefits by encouraging return migration, requires improving labor market conditions back home. Traditional labor market policies aimed at making the local labor market in sending countries more efficient and attractive–especially among highly educated youth in strategic sectors, such as doctors and information and communication technology professionals–can be used for that purpose.

Addressing bottlenecks in domestic labor markets can increase the relative attractiveness of home economies. The analysis in chapter 3 shows that differences in employment protection legislation can affect bilateral migration flows across countries, even after controlling for differences in levels of income and other dimensions. Rigid employment protection legislation in origin countries as opposed to more flexible employment protection regulation in destination countries implies larger bilateral flows. Labor markets with strong employment protection systems may reduce mobility in and out of employment and may also limit the mobility of workers across occupations. Evidence shows that migration has more positive effects in labor markets with more flexible employment protection laws because natives, especially if highly educated, may benefit from occupational upgrades to more complex jobs. In sending regions, less rigidity in employment protection may also facilitate hiring and job promotion, as well as investment inflows and business start-ups, thereby reducing the incentives to emigrate. Therefore, ensuring that employment protection legislation does not discourage job creation, especially at the entry margin, for first-time job seekers, highly skilled youth. and skilled returnees, can potentially reduce the size of skilled migration.

Strengthening home institutions and governance can also reduce incentives to emigrate. The results of the determinants of bilateral migration flows discussed in chapter 3 show that differentials in the levels of corruption between sending and receiving countries can explain bilateral migration flows: in particular, migration occurs from countries with higher levels of corruption toward countries with low levels of corruption, even after controlling for other characteristics such as differences in income or wages. Corruption is often associated with poor meritocracy, weak enforcement of the rule of law, cronyism, and lack of competitiveness: these factors can particularly discourage the high-skilled, who typically pursue jobs and occupations in which careers and wage progressions can reflect individual productivity and ability. Further, high-skilled workers are typically more mobile across countries and are more likely to benefit from better alternative job opportunities abroad thanks to the free movement of labor in the EU. Therefore, countries addressing corruption in both public and private spheres, and investing in improving the quality of governance and public institutions, might be able to reduce, directly or indirectly, the extent of brain drain.

Reinforcing safety nets and welfare systems in sending countries can also contribute to lower emigration rates. The estimates of the drivers of bilateral migration flows in chapter 3 show that differences in the size of the welfare state across countries, measured by social protection expenditures per capita, explain bilateral migration flows, also after controlling for differences in the levels of income and other country-specific characteristics. In line with the theory of "welfare magnets," migration occurs from countries with low per capita social protection expenditures to countries with higher social protection expenditures. Strengthening safety nets in origin countries can therefore deter out-migration, particularly for groups that have a high propensity to leave the country; for instance, youth could benefit from targeted housing subsidies during the first years of their working life (especially young couples), and women could benefit from a larger quantity and better quality of child care services.

Opening domestic labor markets to non-EU countries can help import needed skills, to the extent that doing so is politically feasible. Emigration in several sending regions in the EU can lead to shortages in specific occupations. Increased immigration of professionals who are in high demand from third countries can reduce these shortages and future demographic pressures. Immigration is already a rising phenomenon in parts of the 13 New Member States that joined the EU in 2004, 2007, and 2013 (NMS13), in particular by citizens of non-EU Eastern European countries.[2] Governments can boost immigration by promoting bilateral labor agreements and by easing the hiring of foreign workers among companies in sectors with rising labor demand.

POLICY IMPLICATIONS IN THE MEDIUM TO LONG RUN

In the longer run, countries with high emigration rates have additional policy options available to maximize the benefits of brain circulation and to increase the supply of skills in accordance with needs in the labor market. The main policy options might be divided between those that can be implemented independently and those that need coordination between countries. In terms of content, policies can also be grouped in the following areas: education financing policies, policies aimed at expanding the quality and quantity of education, policies addressing the labor market, policies targeting the reintegration and return of highly skilled migrants, and policies addressing the business environment and ecosystem.

Policies that can be implemented independently by either receiving or sending countries

Reforms on tertiary education financing could be designed to address the fiscal losses associated with the emigration of graduates of publicly funded universities. The mobility of graduates generates free-riding problems in relation to the provision and funding of public education (Gérard and Uebelmesser 2014). Tertiary education financing policies, in addition to public funding, typically include the tuition fees of graduates, student loans or time-based repayment loans, and income-contingent loans (ICLs) (for a review, see Chapman and Higgins 2013). Countries characterized by high tuition fees for tertiary education have introduced government-financed ICLs to ensure access to tertiary education to students from all socioeconomic backgrounds. The rationale for the government to be the guarantor of these loans is an equity principle, that is, to ensure access to education to financially constrained students by addressing market failures in the provision of financing for education from the private sector. The first country to introduce this financing mechanism was Australia (Chapman and Hicks 2018). Other countries using this instrument include Hungary, New Zealand, and the United Kingdom (Chapman and Doan 2019). Unlike regular student loans, whereby students repay the loan in fixed annuity amounts over a predetermined time horizon until the debt is extinguished, students taking out ICLs begin repaying the loans only once their incomes exceed a certain threshold, and the repayment amount is adjusted proportionally depending on the labor incomes of the beneficiaries (Chapman 2006). In some cases, the outstanding amount of ICL debt is absorbed by the state after a certain period, for example, 20–25 years. ICLs may thus embody a progressive element by implicitly subsidizing the payment of tuition fees until a certain level of labor income is reached during the borrower's working life and by entirely exempting low earners.

ICLs may be an appropriate instrument for ensuring access to education, despite costly tuition fees. Such arrangements can also help guarantee the fiscal sustainability of tertiary education within systems in which tertiary education is provided by the private sector, the public sector, or both sectors. However, whether ICLs may be used to limit the drain of human resources in countries with high emigration rates is open to debate. The introduction of tuition fees might, in fact, discourage enrollment in tertiary education in countries of origin, and, given the free mobility of students within the EU, students might decide to emigrate earlier and enroll in universities in countries where tertiary education is still mostly publicly provided and free or available at low cost, for example, in France, Germany, and the Nordic countries. Students might also decide to emigrate despite the option of taking out an ICL, and the enforcement of loan repayments might be compromised if graduates emigrate for long periods or permanently.

As a possible solution to these shortcomings, ICL contracts could be designed to make loan repayments feasible and tax-deductible in destination countries (Poutvaara 2004). This approach would require coordination and bilateral agreements between sending and receiving countries, possibly in the context of the EU's unique labor market with free internal mobility of workers. It would be more compatible with incentives from the standpoint of the emigration of students. Furthermore, it would imply that richer receiving countries would refund some of the education expenditures of the sending countries on the human capital that has been lost. In the absence of bilateral agreements allowing the repayment of ICLs in receiving countries, ICLs should involve regular annuity payments if beneficiaries are residing abroad. Chapman and Higgins (2013) suggest that, in case of emigration, ICL beneficiaries should repay their outstanding debt before leaving the country. A similar modality is currently being adopted in New Zealand.

Another potential advantage of ICLs is that the introduction of tuition fees could help enliven the competition between publicly funded and privately funded universities, thereby improving the overall quality of education in countries of origin. Chapman and Doris (2019) simulate the effects of introducing time-based repayment loans versus various types of ICLs in the case of Ireland, in which the government has attempted to limit the emigration of qualified professionals in the health sector, especially doctors. The authors find that ICLs generally reduce the debt burden relative to standard student loans, especially among low earners, and are also associated with a lower probability of default.

An alternative to ICLs would be the introduction of tuition fees according to a progressive program. Such programs could help avoid discouraging the enrollment of students from disadvantaged socioeconomic backgrounds or from financially constrained households. For graduates who choose to find jobs in their home countries, the tuition fees could be recovered during the first years of working life through general taxation—using, for instance, income tax credits or allowances that would allow the amounts paid in tuition fees to be deducted from taxes over time. Graduates who emigrate would not be able to benefit from the tax credits. Despite addressing the fiscal imbalances involved in highly skilled migration, this solution would not discourage university students from emigrating to study in other countries. Poutvaara (2004, 2008) provides a thorough analysis of the implications of different education financing policies for the mobility of higher education students.

There is also a need to better monitor the skill demand and supply in sending countries and to expand the supply and quality of education in targeted occupations. Improvements in quantity and quality in the provision of skills are essential to preventing labor shortages and accommodating the incentivizing effects of migration on human capital accumulation. Such an approach requires putting in place adequate skill monitoring systems to track the demand and supply for specific skills and anticipate shortages, in particular in critical occupations, to expand education supply in specific fields and occupations in a timely way. Examples of similar demand-driven migration policies can be found in Australia, Canada, and the United Kingdom. Once these needs have been identified, efforts to respond to skill demand can be made at both the intensive margin (by enhancing the capacity of schools and universities) and the extensive margin (by establishing new education centers). It has been shown that education systems typically provide students with skills that are useful in local labor markets but less useful in international labor markets (Poutvaara 2008). The main source of tension is that any increase in the international applicability of education may raise the incentives for students to invest greater effort in acquiring education but reduces the incentives for public sector provision of education. The introduction of a tax on graduates, whereby graduates would be required to pay a share of their future taxes in the country where they received their education, regardless of the country of current residence, has been shown to reduce, though not to eliminate, this problem (Poutvaara 2008).

Introducing fiscal incentives can help attract highly skilled professionals back to the home country. And in the short term, governments can implement tax reductions in specific strategic sectors, such as academia and scientific research. For example, Italy passed Law Decree 34/2019, which introduced new tax incentives for entrepreneurs, researchers, professors, and professional athletes to transfer their tax residency to Italy. The evidence of the effectiveness and sustainability of such programs in the medium to long run, however, is still limited; narrative evidence shows that beneficiaries use the benefits only temporarily and tend to leave the country again once the benefits expire.

Reintegration programs could help smooth the transition of returning migrants into the domestic labor market and support returnees in starting up businesses. Despite the positive wage premiums available to them in the labor market, returnees still face challenges. They tend to have weaker domestic networks upon return compared with those who stayed in the country and, given the higher rates of self-employment and entrepreneurship among returnees, may be negatively affected by administrative and institutional barriers to setting up businesses.

Strengthening the business ecosystems in sending countries can ease the launch of start-ups by return migrants. Sending countries tend to lag in the ease of doing business and in the business regulatory burden compared with migrant-receiving regions in the EU. The business environment affects the start-up of entrepreneurial activities in sending regions and the capacity to attract investments and economic activity. Improvements in this environment may reduce the incentives to emigrate and encourage return migration.

Investing in language programs could also enhance the labor market integration of migrants in receiving countries. Limited command of the host country language among immigrant workers has been evidenced as an important barrier to successful integration in the host labor market. Insufficient language fluency devalues many skills acquired by migrants and is one of the leading reasons behind their higher occupational downgrade. Evidence suggests high returns to language ability in terms of earnings and employability (Bleakley and Chin 2004; Chiswick and Miller 2010; Dustmann and Fabbri 2003); however, at the same time, learning can be costly, particularly for those immigrants who arrive at a later stage of their lives or who stay in ethnic enclaves without much interaction with the local population (Beckhusen et al. 2013). As a consequence, there is a sizable share of the immigrant population in the EU that struggles to master the host country's language.[3] In this context, receiving countries can further invest in language training programs for migrants as part of the broader introductory programs to enhance the integration of labor migrants and to improve the net fiscal balance of migration for the country. Government-led language training for immigrant workers with limited language proficiency in France has been shown to increase the labor force participation of beneficiaries, with larger impacts among more highly educated workers (Lochmann, Rapoport, and Speciale 2019). In Germany, a language training program targeted to unemployment migrants has also been shown to increase employment probability (Lang 2018).

Policies requiring coordination between sending and receiving countries

The assessment of critical skills and occupations can be achieved by building an EU-wide labor demand system. A coordination mechanism is needed to match demand and supply more effectively between sending and receiving regions and to facilitate brain circulation and return migration. In sending countries, education supply targets should reflect a consideration not only of the projected domestic demand in the following years but also of the migrant outflows from specific occupations.

Strengthening ongoing efforts to certify foreign credentials across EU countries can help improve the labor market integration of migrants and enhance mobility. The imperfect recognition of foreign credentials is one of the reasons for the larger occupational downgrade of qualified migrants in host countries (Chiswick and Miller 2009; Tani 2017). Employers often have little information or knowledge about the validity of academic or occupational qualifications acquired abroad, which reduces the value of those credentials. This brain waste comes at a cost for both sending and receiving countries. At the destination, the untapped use of migrants' skills can reduce productivity and tax revenues. Occupational downgrade lowers migrants' earning potential and their subsequent capacity to send remittances back to the origin country. Not using certain higher skills during the migration episode can hinder the ability of migrants to use those skills upon return to the home country. Within EU countries, there have been important efforts to validate foreign education credentials, but significant hurdles persist. According to the EU Labour Force Survey ad hoc migration module in 2014, about 10 percent of high-skilled migrants from the NMS13 living in other EU countries had problems validating their degrees, highlighting the persistence of these barriers within the EU. Further coordination across EU countries to validate foreign credentials will thus enhance labor mobility and the integration of migrants within the EU territory.

Building global skill partnerships between sending and receiving countries would help address losses of human capital and financial burden in the former while ensuring better matches in the latter. Under these bilateral arrangements, the country of origin agrees to train people in skills needed in both origin and destination countries. Among the trainees, some choose to stay and increase human capital in the country of origin whereas others migrate to the country of destination for a period of time. In exchange for receiving migrants with specifically needed skill, the country of destination provides technology and finance for the training. Global skill partnerships address the potential loss of essential human capital in the country of origin while preparing potential migrants for work in the host country (Clemens 2015). In Europe, this approach has already been implemented by Germany, through the German Agency for International Cooperation, with pilots in Kosovo and Morocco.

Promoting the full portability of social protection benefits for migrants can ensure better cost sharing between countries. The lack or incomplete portability of social protection such as health and unemployment insurance and pensions negatively affects migrants' labor market decisions as well as their capacity to cope with social risks during downturns or unexpected health shocks (Holzman and Koettl 2015). It also results in unequal financial burdens and benefits across sending and receiving countries (Werding and McLennan 2011). Although countries within the EU have made progress, such as migrants' full access to health insurance in their country of residence conditional on national legislation, there are no financial transfers between countries (Holzman and Koettl 2015). Therefore, full portability of pensions and health and unemployment insurance will avoid imposing external costs or benefits on other members of the system in the source and destination countries.

Continuing the EU-wide efforts to curb the cost of remittances would also increase the benefit of migration for migrant households. As shown in chapter 5, remittances have quadrupled in the NMS13 as a share of gross domestic product during the last 25 years, providing a vital income supplement to many households. The EU has developed a regulatory environment through the European Payment Service Directive in order to harmonize payments, including remittances, throughout the EU Member States. These efforts have helped reduce the costs of remittances, particularly within the EU. For example, the average transaction cost for a group of bilateral corridors between EU15 and NMS13 countries for which data were available was 5.7 percent in the third quarter of 2020, compared to 6.8 percent in 2015.[4] These costs are lower than the average for non-EU migrant-sending countries. However, the wide variations in remittance costs by sending and receiving countries within the EU leave room for further convergence in prices and overall reduction in prices through the adoption of new technologies and further harmonization of regulatory frameworks.[5]

BETTER-INFORMED POLICIES REQUIRE BETTER DATA COLLECTION ON MIGRATION

Given that most EU migration occurs within the EU, far more detailed and comprehensive data on the internal mobility of individuals are needed. Data on emigration and return migration flows are currently quite limited. Only a few EU-wide ad hoc surveys or survey modules on migration are available—for example, the 2008 and 2014 EU Labor Force Surveys.[6] In the current survey, it is not possible to distinguish between internal and international mobility, and data on the origin of migration are available only by main regional aggregates (for instance, Africa, Asia, and the EU) and not by specific country of origin.

Household surveys in sending countries face even more difficulties in capturing the current extent of emigration—that is, emigrants currently living abroad—because those people cannot be surveyed directly in the sending countries. Only a few ad hoc national surveys in sending countries capture current migrants through questions asking if any household members are temporarily or permanently living in other countries. The EU Labor Force Survey, for example, includes only information on households in the home countries that have a household member working abroad. This is, however, a very restrictive categorization of emigration because it misses entire households that have moved overseas and can lead to a vast underestimation of the extent of emigration in countries where family migration, as opposed to the emigration of one single individual, is common. In addition, questions or modules aimed at capturing return migrants are often poorly designed, are not sufficiently detailed, and in some cases capture only a small number of return migrants.[7] In a handful of sending countries in Europe, such as Albania and Armenia, more comprehensive household surveys dedicated to migration ask detailed questions about current and return migrants in sampled households. Those surveys, however, remain very rare globally and should be systematized across the EU because they currently do not exist for EU countries.

More in-depth, migration-specific surveys with larger sample sizes are also needed to identify migration trajectories across the main corridors and to describe the migration experience and migrants' eventual reintegration into the local economy. Migration has been shown to be often temporary, meaning that migrants return home after some time overseas, including in Europe (Dustmann and Görlach 2016). Currently, available surveys allow for observation of migrants only at a given point in time in either the origin or the destination country, without observing their past migration history and employment outcomes back home. There is a great need for panel data collection following migrants over time or, alternatively, for collecting retrospective information on the entire employment and migration history of current and returning migrants to better understand their migration decisions, trajectories, and contributions to the home economy after returning home. Better data collection is a prerequisite for building an evidence-based, data-driven labor market demand system.

Finally, there is a strong need to better capture cross-country labor mobility in national administrative data sources, and to integrate them within and across countries. A handful of destination countries in Europe, mainly Scandinavian countries and the Netherlands, have put together comprehensive administrative data sets covering the entire population and recording the arrival and departure of immigrants. Such initiatives allow for the precise measurement of the magnitude and composition of migrant inflows and for the capture of temporary movement. They require not only that administrative or registry data be collected and made available but also that they can be matched with other data sets containing additional variables, such as labor market outcomes. In addition, procedures must be in place that record the immigrants' length of residence or departure date, which is not the case for every country. Such initiatives need to be generalized across countries in the EU. Some of these register data sets also include information about the destination country in addition to the date of exit, providing an opportunity to track migrants across national borders. Such tracking, however, requires tight cross-country collaboration and agreements allowing workers to be linked across national administrative databases, which are currently very rare. One exception is the merger of the Finnish and Swedish population registers to study emigrant and returnee selection among Finns going to Sweden. Such initiatives need to be generalized to other relevant migration corridors within the EU. In addition, sending countries need systematic data collection on migrants leaving the country. Such administrative databases on emigrants should allow the tracking of workers in and out of the country through the use of unique individual identifiers, allowing the database to capture the return of workers to the home country as well as repeated migration.

NOTES

1. See Article 45, "Charter of Fundamental Rights of the European Union," Document 12012P /TXT, EUR-Lex (database), Publications Office of the European Union, Luxembourg, https://eur-lex.europa.eu/eli/treaty/char_2012/oj.

2. The NMS13 (with year of accession) consists of the following: Cyprus, the Czech Republic, Estonia, Hungary, Latvia, Lithuania, Malta, Poland, the Slovak Republic, and Slovenia (2004); Bulgaria and Romania (2007); and Croatia (2013).

3. According to the EU Labour Force Survey migration module of 2014, about one-third of migrants in the EU has at most an intermediate level in the host language.

4. Based on the World Bank Remittance Prices Worldwide database, available at http://remittanceprices.worldbank.org. The EU15's full membership before 2004 consisted of Austria, Belgium, Denmark, Finland, France, Germany, Greece, Ireland, Italy, Luxembourg, the Netherlands, Portugal, Spain, Sweden, and the United Kingdom.

5. For example, transaction costs accounted for 9.8 percent of total transfers between Germany and Hungary but only 3.4 percent between Romania and Spain.

6. See EU Labour Force Survey (database), Eurostat, European Commission, Luxembourg, https://ec.europa.eu/eurostat/statistics-explained/index.php/EU_labour_force_survey.

7. Typically, surveys ask whether individuals worked overseas in recent years; such questions capture only a small sample of return migrants in surveys with a limited total sample size or with a limited incidence of return migration.

REFERENCES

Beckhusen, Julia, Raymond J. G. M. Florax, Thomas de Graaff, Jacques Poot, and Brigitte Waldorf. 2013. "Living and Working in Ethnic Enclaves: Language Proficiency of Immigrants in U.S. Metropolitan Areas." *Papers in Regional Science* 92 (2): 305–28.

Bleakley, Hoyt, and Aimee Chin. 2004. "Language and Earnings: Evidence from Childhood Immigrants." *Review of Economics and Statistics* 86 (2): 481–96.

Chapman, Bruce. 2006. "Income Contingent Loans for Higher Education: International Reforms." In *Handbook of the Economics of Education*, vol. 2, edited by Eric A. Hanushek and Finis Welch, 1435–1503. Amsterdam: Elsevier North-Holland.

Chapman, Bruce, and Dung Doan. 2019. "Higher Education Financing: Student Loans." *Economics of Education Review* 71 (August): 1–6.

Chapman, Bruce, and Aedin Doris. 2019. "Modelling Higher Education Financing Reform for Ireland." *Economics of Education Review* 71 (August): 109–19.

Chapman, Bruce, and Timothy Hicks. 2018. "The Political Economy of the Higher Education Contribution Scheme." In *Handbook on the Politics of Higher Education*, edited by Brendan Cantwell, Hamish Coates, and Roger King, 248–64. Cheltenham, UK: Edward Elgar.

Chapman, Bruce, and Tim Higgins. 2013. "The Costs of Unpaid Higher Education Contribution Scheme Debts of Graduates Working Abroad." *Australian Economic Review* 46 (3): 286–99.

Chiswick, Barry R., and Paul W. Miller. 2009. "The International Transferability of Immigrants' Human Capital." *Economics of Education Review* 28 (2): 162–69.

Chiswick, Barry R., and Paul W. Miller. 2010. "Occupational Language Requirements and the Value of English in the US Labor Market." *Journal of Population Economics* 23 (1): 353–72.

Clemens, Michael A. 2015. "Global Skill Partnerships: A Proposal for Technical Training in a Mobile World." *IZA Journal of Labor Policy* 4, article no. 2.

Dustmann, Christian, and Francesca Fabri. 2003. "Language Proficiency and Labour Market Performance of Immigrants in the UK." *Economic Journal* 113 (489): 695–717.

Dustmann, C., and J. S. Görlach. 2016. "The Economics of Temporary Migrations." *Journal of Economic Literature* 54 (1): 98–136.

Gérard, Marcel, and Silke Uebelmesser, eds. 2014. *The Mobility of Students and the Highly Skilled: Implications for Education Financing and Economic Policy*. CESifo Seminar Series. Cambridge, MA: MIT Press.

Holzmann, Robert, and Johannes Koettl. 2015. "Portability of Pension, Health, and Other Social Benefits: Facts, Concepts, and Issues." *CESifo Economic Studies* 61 (2): 377–415.

Lang, J. 2018. "Employment Effects of Language Training for Unemployed Immigrants." IAB-Discussion Paper 21/2018, Institute for Employment Research, German Federal Employment Agency, Nuremburg.

Lochmann, A., H. Rapoport, and B. Speciale. 2019. "The Effect of Language Training on Immigrants' Economic Integration: Empirical Evidence from France." *European Economic Review* 113 (C): 265–96.

Poutvaara, Panu. 2004. "Educating Europe: Should Public Education Be Financed with Graduate Taxes or Income-Contingent Loans?" *CESifo Economic Studies* 50 (4): 663–84.

Poutvaara, Panu. 2008. "Public and Private Education in an Integrated Europe: Studying to Migrate and Teaching to Stay?" *Scandinavian Journal of Economics* 110 (3): 591–608.

Tani, Massimiliano. 2017. "Local Signals and the Returns to Foreign Education." *Economics of Education Review* 61: 174–90.

Werding, Martin, and Stuart McLennan. 2011. "International Portability of Health-Cost Coverage: Concepts and Experience." SP Discussion Paper 1115, World Bank, Washington, DC.

World Bank. 2018. *Moving for Prosperity: Global Migration and Labor Markets*. Policy Research Report. Washington, DC: World Bank.

Methodology to Estimate Migrants' Return Rates in the European Union

Estimates of the share of migrants who return to their home countries (returnees) are based on a compiled data set of the stock of migrants and returnees in 24 European Union (EU) countries of origin (which include the EU28, less Denmark, Germany, Ireland, and the Netherlands because of a lack of data), 223 receiving countries across the world, and three levels of educational attainment among migrants: low (below upper-secondary education), medium (upper-secondary education completed), and high (tertiary education).[1]

The outcome of interest is the number of returnees in each cell. Data on the bilateral stock of migrants by educational attainment are obtained from the Organisation for Economic Co-operation and Development (OECD) Database on Immigrants in OECD and Non-OECD Countries (DIOC) for 2010/11, based on census data in receiving countries.[2] Data on the stock of returnees are derived from the ad hoc EU Labour Force Survey (LFS) module on migration in 2014, which asked respondents if they had lived in a third country for more than six months during the previous 10 years.[3] All cells that have zeroes in the number of either migrants or returnees are replaced by 1 to allow them to be transformed into logarithms without losing information. A gravity-type equation is estimated that includes control variables typically used in the migration literature and obtained from the CEPII bilateral database, as follows:[4]

$$logreturnees_{ode} = \alpha + \beta*logmigrants_{ode} + \gamma_1*logdistance_{od}$$
$$+ \gamma_2*contig_{od} + \gamma_3*ethnic_{od} + \delta_o + \varphi_d + \varepsilon_{ode}, \qquad (A.1)$$

where $logreturnees_{ode}$ is the logarithm of returnees to the country of origin o from the destination country d; $logmigrants_{ode}$ is the logarithm of migrants from country o in country d; $logdistance$ is the distance in logarithms between the origin and destination countries; $contig$ is a dummy if the two countries are contiguous; $ethnic$ is the share of the population in sending and receiving countries that has a common ethnic background; δ_o are country-of-origin fixed effects; and φ_d are destination-country fixed effects.[5] The regression is estimated using the Poisson pseudo-maximum likelihood estimator (PPML), which is typically used in gravity models of migration (Santos Silva and Tenreyro 2006).

Table A.1 shows the regression results separated for each education level and by different levels of disaggregation of the regions of origin and destination. (β coefficients are allowed to vary for different groups of migrants depending on the regions of origin and destination.) In all specifications, geographic factors and social ties are correlated with the rate of return. The larger the distance traveled by a migrant, the lower the share of migrants who return. Similarly, migration to a neighboring country is associated with a higher likelihood of return. By education level, these effects are larger among less highly skilled

TABLE A.1 Gravity equation of returnees

VARIABLE	(1) PPML LOW EDUCATION	(2) PPML MID EDUCATION	(3) PPML HIGH EDUCATION	(4) PPML LOW EDUCATION	(5) PPML MID EDUCATION	(6) PPML HIGH EDUCATION	(7) PPML LOW EDUCATION	(8) PPML MID EDUCATION	(9) PPML HIGH EDUCATION
Log migrants	0.806**	0.893***	0.961***						
	(0.050)	(0.048)	(0.040)						
Log migrants EU15 origin				0.753***	0.865***	0.949***			
				(0.054)	(0.053)	(0.043)			
Log migrants NMS origin				0.873***	0.914***	0.839***			
				(0.056)	(0.054)	(0.050)			
Log migrants EU15 origin in EU15 destination							0.750***	0.802***	0.968***
							(0.067)	(0.069)	(0.065)
Log migrants EU15 origin in NMS destination							1.051***	1.052***	1.116***
							(0.116)	(0.097)	(0.064)
Log migrants EU15 origin in RoW							0.738***	0.839***	0.898***
							(0.061)	(0.055)	(0.043)
Log migrants NMS origin in EU15 destination							0.791***	0.835***	0.835***
							(0.061)	(0.065)	(0.065)
Log migrants NMS origin in NMS destination							0.906***	0.990***	0.925***
							(0.113)	(0.091)	(0.066)
Log migrants NMS origin in RoW							0.601***	0.788***	0.681***
							(0.075)	(0.068)	(0.050)
Log distance	-0.438**	-0.337**	-0.309***	-0.465**	-0.358**	-0.266**	-0.609***	-0.532***	-0.285***
	(0.221)	(0.157)	(0.102)	(0.198)	(0.159)	(0.110)	(0.191)	(0.154)	(0.107)
Contiguity	-0.155	-0.488***	-0.447***	-0.153	-0.501***	-0.439***	-0.216	-0.548***	-0.431***
	(0.205)	(0.163)	(0.121)	(0.193)	(0.162)	(0.121)	(0.180)	(0.159)	(0.123)
Common ethnic group	-29.477***	-21.228***	-15.179***	-29.756***	-21.054***	-14.795***	-21.675***	-18.044***	-12.282***
	(6.052)	(4.926)	(5.566)	(6.198)	(4.961)	(5.505)	(6.820)	(4.360)	(5.870)
Constant	3.699***	2.162	3.081***	4.146**	2.013	2.534***	5.468***	4.270***	2.355**
	(1.878)	(1.393)	(0.847)	(1.868)	(1.449)	(0.935)	(1.963)	(1.536)	(1.090)
Observations	5,220	5,122	5,056	5,220	5,122	5,056	5,220	5,122	5,056
R²	0.897	0.932	0.962	0.909	0.933	0.962	0.911	0.931	0.963
Country origin FE	YES	YES	YES	YES	YES	YES	YES	YES	YES
Country destination FE	YES	YES	YES	YES	YES	YES	YES	YES	YES

Source: World Bank calculations based on data from the CEPII Gravity Database, the Database on Immigrants in OECD Countries (DIOC) 2010/11 of the Organisation for Economic Co-operation and Development (OECD), and the European Union Labour Force Survey ad-hoc migration module of 2014, Eurostat.

Note: EU15 = full European Union membership before 2004 (Austria, Belgium, Denmark, Finland, France, Germany, Greece, Ireland, Italy, Luxembourg, the Netherlands, Portugal, Spain, Sweden, and the United Kingdom); FE = fixed effects; NMS13 = New Member States joining the EU in 2004 (Cyprus, the Czech Republic, Estonia, Hungary, Latvia, Lithuania, Malta, Poland, the Slovak Republic, and Slovenia), 2007 (Bulgaria and Romania), and 2013 (Croatia); PPML = Poisson pseudo- maximum likelihood; RoW = rest of the world. Robust standard errors in parentheses.

*** $p < 0.01$, ** $p < 0.05$, * $p < 0.1$

workers than among highly educated workers. Regarding ethnic ties, migrants who reside in a country with common ethnic groups with the country of origin (such as Bulgarian Turks in Turkey or Russian Estonians in the Russian Federation) are significantly less likely to return, suggesting that migration motivated for ethnic reasons is usually more permanent.

The coefficients listed in table A.1 for log migrants provide the elasticity of return migration, that is, the percentage increase in returnees by 2014 derived from a 1 percent increase in the stock of emigrants in 2010. Regressions 1–3 include all regions of origin in the EU and destination countries. Regressions 4–6 differentiate the elasticity for migrants from the EU15 (log migrants EU15 origin) and the 13 New Member States, or NMS13 (log migrants NMS origin).[6] Regressions 7–9 provide separate elasticities for EU15 migrants who lived in other EU15 countries (log migrants EU15 origin in EU15 destination), in the NMS13 (log migrants EU15 origin in NMS destination), or in the rest of the world (log migrants EU15 origin in RoW) and migrants from the NMS13 who lived in the EU15 (log migrants NMS origin in EU15 destination), other NMS13 countries (log migrants NMS origin in NMS destination), or in the rest of the world (log migrants NMS origin in RoW).

The migrants' return rates used in the main text (figure 5.12) are then calculated using the following:

$$\text{Migrants' return} = (\text{Returnees} * \text{elasticity}_{r/m}) / (\text{Stock Migrants}) \qquad (A.2)$$

NOTES

1. The EU28 represents the full EU membership before the departure of the United Kingdom in 2020 (Brexit).
2. See DIOC, reference years 2010/11, OECD, Paris, https://www.oecd.org/els/mig/dioc.htm.
3. See "2014 Labour Market Situation of Migrants and Their Immediate Descendants," LFS Ad Hoc Module, EU-LFS (database), Eurostat, European Commission, Luxembourg, https://ec.europa.eu/eurostat/statistics-explained/index.php/EU_labour_force_survey.
4. See CEPII Gravity Database, Centre d'Etudes Prospectives et d'Informations Internationales, Paris, http://www.cepii.fr/cepii/en/bdd_modele/presentation.asp?id=8.
5. In other specifications, dummies are also included for common language, common legal system, and historical ties between the sending and receiving countries; but the coefficients are not statistically significant.
6. The EU15's full membership before 2004 consisted of Austria, Belgium, Denmark, Finland, France, Germany, Greece, Ireland, Italy, Luxembourg, the Netherlands, Portugal, Spain, Sweden, and the United Kingdom. The NMS13 (with year of accession) consists of the following: Cyprus, the Czech Republic, Estonia, Hungary, Latvia, Lithuania, Malta, Poland, the Slovak Republic, and Slovenia (2004); Bulgaria and Romania (2007); and Croatia (2013).

REFERENCE

Santos Silva, J. M. C., and Silvana Tenreyro. 2006. "The Log of Gravity." *Review of Economics and Statistics* 88 (4): 641–58.

Methodology to Estimate the Determinants of Bilateral Migration Flows in the European Union

In the migration gravity equation estimated with results reported in table 3.1, the outcome variable of interest is the log of migration flows from sending country i to receiving country j in year t, for all EU28 and European Free Trade Association countries between 2008 and 2018. The gravity-type, country-pair-specific variables include the population-weighted distance and the time zone differences between the two countries, the size of the countries, and dummy variables indicating a common border, a common language, and a common religion. The regressions also include different potential drivers related to both the labor market and income differentials (gross domestic product per capita, nominal net earnings, inflation rates, and unemployment rates), the economic structure of countries (the value added of the agricultural, manufacturing, and services sectors in total gross domestic product), the legal framework and regulations (the right to work for migrants in the destination country, employment protection legislation, and product market regulations), the depth of the welfare system, and the openness of countries (the share of trade in total gross domestic product). These factors are all introduced as the log of the ratio between receiving country j and sending country i. This is motivated by the fact that is the difference in the values of these variables, rather than the absolute levels per se, that matters in the migration decision. All regressions also include time fixed effects and robust standard errors.

www.ingramcontent.com/pod-product-compliance
Lightning Source LLC
Chambersburg PA
CBHW041448210326
41599CB00004B/177